...TON & COURTS MILLS

CRADLE BRIDGE MILL

WOOLLEN MILLS *of* TROWBRIDGE

Alan Andrew

WARP AND WEFT

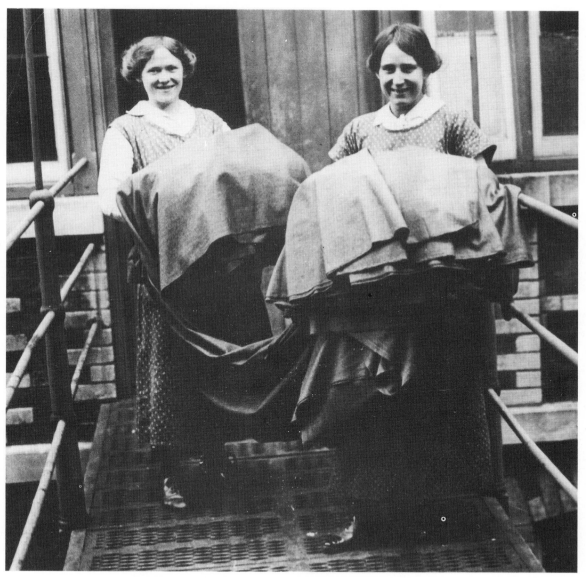

FRONT COVER: Menders, Salters, Trowbridge 1913. (WRO)

Studley Mill, Trowbridge, 1860, with chimney stack, 1878.

WARP and WEFT

The Somerset and Wiltshire woollen industry

BY

KENNETH H. ROGERS FSA

Drawings by
ALAN ANDREW

BARRACUDA BOOKS LIMITED
BUCKINGHAM, ENGLAND
MCMLXXXVI

PUBLISHED BY BARRACUDA BOOKS LIMITED
BUCKINGHAM, ENGLAND
AND PRINTED BY
HEFFERS PRINTERS LIMITED
CAMBRIDGE, ENGLAND

BOUND BY
CAMELOT PRESS plc
SOUTHAMPTON, ENGLAND

JACKET PRINTED BY
CHENEY & SONS LIMITED
BANBURY, OXON

PHOTOLITHOGRAPHY BY
CAMERA GRAPHICS LIMITED
AMERSHAM, ENGLAND

TEXT SET IN BASKERVILLE BY
GRAHAM BURN TYPESETTING
LEIGHTON BUZZARD, ENGLAND

© Kenneth H. Rogers 1986

ISBN 0 86023 264 6

Contents

ACKNOWLEDGEMENTS 8

FOREWORD BY KENNETH HUDSON 9

PREFACE BY JOHN NAISH 9

THE WEAVERS' TURN-OUT 10

BACK CLOTH 12

INDUSTRIAL DAWN 17

THE GOLDEN AGE 23

SPANISH WOOL AND DUTCHMEN 31

RICH MAN, POOR MAN 38

EXTREME GOOD GOODS 46

WHAT ABOUT THE WORKERS? 62

MAN AND MACHINE 67

WONDERFULLY IMPROVED 73

HARD TIMES 99

INDIAN SUMMER 109

THE FINAL CURTAIN 119

WARP AND WEFT 128

BIBLIOGRAPHY 139

INDEX 140

SUBSCRIBERS 143

Acknowledgements

My interest in the woollen industry first arose almost 40 years ago, when the firms of J. and T. Clark and Samuel Salter were kind enough to employ me in school holidays and university vacations. Ken Ponting, managing director of Salters and later director of the Pasold Research Fund for the Study of Textile History, encouraged me to work on the history of the buildings used in the industry, and it is a great sadness to me that neither he nor Julia de Lacy Mann have lived to see this book, which relies to a considerable degree on their published work. I have, however, used most of the primary sources myself, and a good deal of new material is presented here. Readers will see from the Bibliography that the Somerset industry has been less worked on than that of Wiltshire; Michael McGarvie and Joe Bettey both helped to redress the balance, by passing on material from their own researches.

The museums at Devizes, Trowbridge, Chippenham, and Frome and the Bradford-on-Avon Preservation Trust all provided illustrations from their collections; acknowledgements to other friends who lent or took photographs are made in the captions. Thanks are due to the Directors of Library Services in the three counties of Wiltshire, Somerset, and Avon for help with subscription arrangements.

As on a previous occasion, Ann Mattock typed the text from a hand-written draft with great precision. Alan Andrew has been a tower of strength in processing films and printing photographs, as well as in his own artistic field.

Key to Caption Credits

AA	Alan Andrew
AP	Adrian Powell
BM	B. Mitchell
BPT	Bradford Preservation Trust
CB	Clive Birch
CDC	Dr C.D. Lycett
CM	Chippenham Museum
DM	Devizes Museum
DP	D. Pollard
FM	Frome Museum
SPC	Seend CE Primary School
TM	Trowbridge Museum
WLMS	Wiltshire Library and Museum Service
WRO	Wiltshire Record Office

Foreword

by Kenneth Hudson

With *The Book of Trowbridge,* published two years ago, Ken Rogers achieved an effective combination of pictures and text which clearly deserved to be repeated, and almost the greatest praise that one can give to his second book is to say that it is as good as his first. For generations the manufacture of woollen cloth was at the centre of the pattern of life in Wiltshire and Somerset, and its steady disappearance during the past 150 years has left a social and economic gap which has never been adequately filled.

By putting his emphasis on the human aspects of the rise and fall of this once great industry, Ken Rogers has guaranteed his readers an interesting book, but at the same time made his task more difficult because, although pictures of mill exteriors are relatively abundant, photographs of workers and machinery are not easy to find. The fact that *Warp and Weft* has such a generous and well-balanced supply of illustrations is a great triumph for the author. By providing an opportunity for the millworkers to emerge from the shadows and to become real people, he has brought life into the story and helped the statistics to make sense. We should be very grateful to him.

Kenneth Hudson.

Preface

by John Naish of E.V. Naish Ltd of Wilton

In the early 19th century my ancestor William Naish was a cloth manufacturer in Wilton. His son William changed the business to the production of felt, and the firm now makes pressed felt for a wide variety of industrial purposes. Since the closure of Salter's factory at Trowbridge in 1982, E.V. Naish Ltd is the only survivor of the local firms which were once active in the wool textile industry, while a further link with the past is provided by my firm's continuing use of fulling stocks, a technology introduced in the 12th century. I look forward to learning more of the Wiltshire and Somerset woollen industry from this latest research by Ken Rogers, which I believe will make a notable contribution to recording its history.

The Weavers' Turn-Out

O, hark! my lads, and give an ear, to listen unto me,
A story unto you I'll relate which happen'd the other day,
It's concerning of weavers, who for their rights maintain,
We have been labouring many a year, but still it was all in vain.

CHORUS - So let us all, while in our bloom,
     Drink success to the weavers' loom.

In Dursley town in Gloucestershire, for wages we stood out,
It was for one 3-pence per yard on a chain of broad cloth,
Our clubs we have to support our wives and children dear,
We live in hopes of better times while we drink a jug of beer.

Look all around the neighbourhood and you will quickly hear,
We are in hopes our employers our wages will ensure,
For provisions they are plentiful, they are so rich and good,
And so my boys we'll never fear our clubs they will stand good.

Behold the town of Bratford and Wotton-under-hedge too,
The weavers they are all combin'd to their colors will stand true,
The town of Trowbridge as you hear, and not leave Milsom out,
And all round the neighbourhood for wages will stand out.

All round the neighbourhood the trade it has been good,
For all mechanics in the trade to support themselves with food,
But the weavers they are valiant men as you will understand,
Then for our wages we stand out and no more be at command.

So to conclude my ditty and to finish up my song,
We'll drink success to the weavers, may the trade be carried on.
Likewise to our employers wherever they may dwell,
May the trade be in a flourishing state, and never for to fail.

Bonner & Henson, Printers,
No 3, Narrow Wine Street, Bristol

Broadside poem on the strike of 1829

'Labour is the source of wealth' proclaimed this 1822 Weavers' Union mug –
probably from the competitive north, it presaged the organisation six years
later of the workforce in the south west. (CB)

11

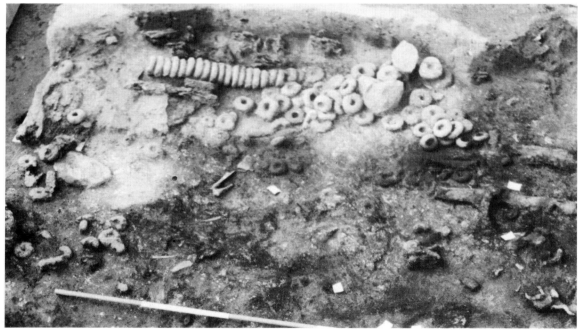

ABOVE: Spinning with the spindle. BELOW: Weights of a vertical loom in
the ruins of a burnt Saxon house, Swindon. (WLMS)

Backcloth

The subject of this book is the history of the making of cloth in west Wiltshire and east Somerset, a district which formed the southern sector of the area where high-quality cloths, recently known as 'West of England', were made. In this district and in Gloucestershire the industry assumed a position of national importance in the later Middle Ages, which it retained to some degree until the turn of the present century. It finally died out in our district in 1982, but cloth is still produced as yet in the Stroud district of Gloucestershire.

Cloth has been made from wool at least since the Bronze Age, and evidence of weaving in Saxon times has been found at many places in Wiltshire and Somerset. The cloth produced was no doubt for a local market, and its making simple, compared with more complex processes of later times. How a Saxon craftsman turned wool into cloth is the starting point of the story, which necessarily follows changing techniques.

There are four groups of processes: the preparation of the wool, the conversion of wool to yarn, the weaving of the yarn to form cloth, and the finishing of the cloth to make it hard-wearing and of good appearance and feel.

For the first, our Saxon would have scoured the wool, probably by warming it in a solution made from the soap-wort plant, or in water and urine, and then suspending it in a running stream to rinse it, drying it in the sun. Then he would have picked it over, and probably beaten it with rods, to get out embedded dirt and burrs. The wool was then made ready for working by adding oil or grease.

The actual making of the yarn consisted of two processes: combing the wool with an iron comb to lay the fibres parallel, and then spinning it, by using a wooden or bone spindle, fitted with a circular whorl at the lower end to act as a flywheel. This simple device enabled the combed wool to be drawn out into a fine yarn, which gained the necessary strength from the twist imparted to it, by the spinning of the spindle, as it was allowed to fall from the spinner's hands to the ground. She would then pick it up and wind the yarn on to it produced by one drop, before starting again. When the spindle was full, the yarn had to be wound into a ball.

To make his cloth the Saxon weaver would have used a warp-weighted vertical loom. Such a loom consisted of a rectangular wooden frame, arranged in an almost vertical position, from the top bar of which the warp (or lengthwise threads) hang, kept in tension by stone or earthenware weights, tied to the lower ends of bundles of threads. Alternate threads are arranged in different ways; one group, say even numbers, always remain on the weaver's side of the loom, sloping slightly towards him from the top bar, to rest against another one at the lower end, just above the weights. The other group, odd numbers, at the start of the weaving, hang vertically from the top bar almost to the floor, so dangling on the side of the loom furthest from the weaver. At this point the first weft (breadthwise) thread is inserted, and pushed hard to the top bar by means of a wooden rod. It is now necessary to pull the odd threads to the loom nearer to the weaver, before inserting the second weft thread; this is accomplished by having a rod parallel to the ground at a central point, to which the odd threads are attached by loops of string, called heddles. By pulling this rod towards him, the weaver brings the central part of each odd thread nearer to him than the even threads, and at this point the weft thread is passed back and again beaten upwards. Such a loom would weave a simple plain cloth, and twills could be woven by the use of more than one heddle-rod.

Finishing of the cloth would have begun with scouring, to free it of the added oil and any dirt picked up in spinning and weaving. For better qualities this was followed by raising a nap on the cloth, by using a wooden implement set with spikes or teazles, then by shearing the nap close, and even by using large iron shears, finally by pressing in a screw press.

Dyeing could be done at one of several stages, but would generally have been in the wool, if a patterned cloth was to be produced, or of the cloth for a plain colour.

Such methods would have persisted into early mediaeval times, when we first know of the production of cloth for a wider market in our area. Our knowledge comes from only two references: in the late twelfth century 'The Laws of the Weavers and Fullers of Marlborough' were copied into a book of the laws and customs of London, and in 1218 at Marlborough and Bedwyn makers of cloths called burels obtained exemption from the provisions of Magna Carta, regarding the minimum width of woollen cloth. The laws show that the weavers and fullers were mere workpeople, who strictly controlled entry into the ranks of freemen who ran the industry, and we know from other sources that burel was a low-quality cloth, suitable for clothing soldiers, or being given in alms to the poor.

This obscure industry in the east of Wiltshire was in time succeeded by one which produced cloth of a higher quality. Cloth produced as described was made from unsorted wool, combining most, if not all, of the lengths and qualities available from one sheep or flock, which had been combed to lay the fibres parallel. Combing would have removed any short wool. In the 13th century we first hear of a method of preparing wool for spinning by the use of cards – boards set with a uniform covering of small wires, held by means of projecting handles. The carder works a small quantity of wool between a card held in each hand, to produce a small roll from which the yarn can be spun. Carding mixes and crosses the wool fibres, so that the yarn is characteristically soft and hairy. Its application to shorter wool sorted from the fleeces, leaving longer wool only to be combed, introduced the two basic sections of the wool cloth industry which still exist today – *woollen* goods made from carded wool, and *worsted* goods made from combed wool.

The second innovation was the introduction of the spinning wheel – not the more familiar wheel with treadle and flyer, but the spindle or great wheel, whereby the spinner stands, operating the wheel with one hand, and paying out prepared wool from the other, so that it is spun by the rapidly-revolving spindle driven by a belt from the wheel. The length of one spinning is virtually the same as with the simple spindle, since the spinner cannot move out of reach of the wheel; at this point she has to stop the wheel, move the yarn from the tip of the spindle nearer to its base, and then turn the wheel again to wind the new length on. This wheel, which enabled yarn to be spun more rapidly, appeared in England in the 14th century, and was the one used to make woollen yarn in our district, as long as hand spinning continued.

Although a loom similar to the type still used by hand weavers today may have been known in late Roman times, it is clear from weights discovered that the vertical loom was the common one until the early Middle Ages. It was then generally superseded by the more efficient horizontal kind, in which a warp of great length can be wound on a horizontal revolving beam. From the warp beam, the threads pass horizontally to the weaving position, where a series of harnesses containing heddles can be moved up and down, worked by foot pedals, so that the opening in the warp threads (the shed) can be varied to a degree not possible with a simpler loom. The weaver passes through the weft thread, using a shuttle, and beats it in, using a comb (called a slay in the west), which is suspended from the top of the loom. As cloth is made, it can be wound forward on to another beam in front of the weaver. Two weavers can use such looms to make double width, or broad cloth, one throwing the shuttle through to the other.

The fourth innovation has recently been re-appraised. We have already heard of the fullers of Marlborough; we can picture them at work, standing on the cloth in a trough, and treading it with bare feet in water and a detergent, probably the fuller's earth which takes its name from the process. (Reliefs of this can be seen at Pompeii.) Until recently it was assumed that this was partly to scour out the oil added to the wool, but principally to shrink the cloth and cause it to felt, making the individual threads forming the cloth disappear. But this may not have been achieved until the mechanisation of fulling which, though known in Italy in the 10th cenuty, did not appear here until the late 11th.

Fulling stocks: the near stock is being lifted by a tappet, and will be allowed to fall on to the cloth as the wheel goes on. The far stock has fallen on to the cloth and will be lifted by the next tappet.

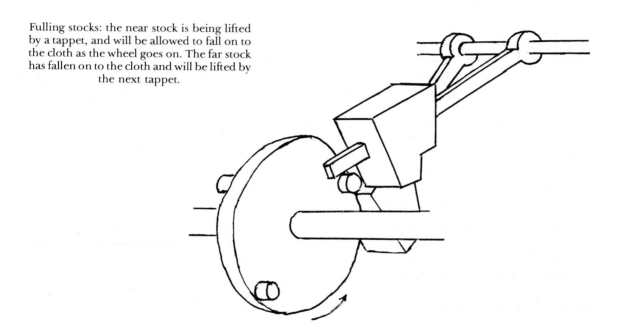

The action of a fulling mill is simple enough; two heavy wooden hammers, called stocks, are pivoted at a point a short distance from the ends of their shafts. Short lengths of the shafts project through the stocks, and are placed so that they are raised by tappets, projecting laterally from the rim of a revolving wheel, so raising the stocks. As the tappets move on, they disengage from the shafts, and so allow the raised hammers to fall on to the cloth, pounding it in a far more effective way than human feet. The tappet wheel, being fixed to a shaft turned by water power, would enable the process to be kept up for long periods, generating considerable heat; a cloth heavily fulled in this way could shrink by a third of its length and more than a quarter of its width.

The introduction of the fulling mill into England was described by the late Professor Carus-Wilson as 'an industrial revolution of the 13th century'; the decline of the old fine cloth industry in such centres as Lincoln, Beverley and York was due to re-location in areas where water-power was more easily available, such as the west country and Yorkshire; that incidentally freed the craftsmen from regulation by town guilds. If this was right, the decline of the 13th century was illusory. Cloth was being made, but more and more in the country. Her ideas, firmly-stated, produced reactions;

the first brought new evidence of an overall decline in the 13th century. More recently, Dr A.R. Bridbury has suggested in *Medieval English Clothmaking*, that both views are wrong – that the making of cloth from wool was widespread in town and country, though we know more about the towns. He sees no reason why mills could not be built in the populous east and rightly points out that the greatest concentration of early mills was in South Wales and Cornwall, never noted for commercial cloth production. He suggests foot-fulling continued in a chronically over-populated country, where labour-saving devices were more likely to have raised than lowered costs.

Now A.R. Hall and N.C. Russell (in their article 'What about the Fulling-Mill?') doubt whether foot-fulling could ever have achieved the results, in terms of shrinkage and felting, which the stocks could. The purpose of foot-fulling, was to do in our area what was later called braying, that is to scour the grease and dirt out of the cloth, a process done later by the stocks, driven 'leisurely and without such violence as heats'. They question whether foot-fulling could ever have produced the violent reaction caused by the motion of the stocks over many hours, generating considerable heat and thereby the great shrinkage and felting of the cloth.

Hall and Russell believe that the fulling mill was one of a 'parcel of technical innovations' – carding, the spinning wheel, and the horizontal loom – which enabled woollen cloth proper to be made, and ultimately divided the industry into its two classic branches of woollens and worsteds. The characteristic cloth produced by fulling was broadcloth, made at first at least partly, and later fully, from carded wool, heavily felted and finished by raising a nap and then shearing it. This cloth, heavier than any overcoating made today, became a much-sought product, and may well have been the reason for the re-location of the industry in our area of abundant water-power.

Carding, and spinning on the great wheel.

16

Industrial Dawn

The development of the local broadcloth industry may go back to the late 12th century, with a fulling mill on the Marden at Stanley recorded in 1189. In the next century there were other Wiltshire mills at Downton, and at Elcot near Marlborough (both 1294), West Harnham (1299) and Mere (before 1300). The mill at Elcot was rebuilt for the King by the Constable of Marlborough in 1237–8, and detailed accounts include payments for making the *flagella et baterella*, the stocks themselves. The existence of four mills close to Salisbury suggests that clothmaking formed an important occupation in the new city. Early in the next century there was a mill on the Kennet at Chilton Foliat below Marlborough, so that borough too probably remained a centre. There was a mill at Weston on the Avon below Bath in 1296.

Other than these, 13th century evidence is limited to a scatter of names; Adam le Folur, whose son was killed by the wheel of a mill at Bradford before 1249, offers the first indication of an industry which was to find its heartland in west Wiltshire. Another fuller named John lived at Lullington on the River Frome c1300. But 13th century England was noted chiefly for the export of wool to the great clothmaking centres of Flanders and Italy. It was in the reign of Edward III that English clothmaking grew into a great export industry, helped (incidentally) by the King's manipulation and taxation of wool exports as part of his war effort.

By the end of the 14th century, Salisbury had become an important centre, as is borne out by the returns of the aulnager, a Royal official who had to measure cloths put up for sale, to make sure that they conformed to the statutory assize; if they did, he affixed a lead seal, and charged duty at 4d a cloth; if not, they were confiscated. For much of the later part of the century the Wiltshire aulnage was let; significantly the rent rose from £60 a year in 1362 to £86 13s 4d in 1390. In 1394–5, when the aulnage was collected directly, 5,039 cloths were listed under suburbs, compared to 723 for the rest of the country. For 1395–6, 1397–8, 1398–9, the Salisbury figures are 6,749, 7,044 and 4,030.

A correlation of the aulnage return of 1396–7 with lists of householders living in the four wards of the city in 1399 or 1400 shows that the aulnage return is genuine (some are known to be fabricated); that 83 per cent of the names on it were Salisbury householders; that 27 per cent of all Salisbury householders had cloth aulnaged, to an average of 24 cloths per householder. Named occupations in the ward lists include 45 weavers, 15 fullers, and 10 dyers, but many have no stated occupation. The number of fullers who could not have had mills in the city is a warning that the word (or its local equivalent, tucker) was frequently used to describe a general finisher of cloth, witness the frequent occurrence of tucker's shears.

Three types of cloth were made in Salisbury, all apparently of a middle price range – plain coloured broadcloths, striped cloths called rays, and narrow coloured cloths called osetes. Rays too were narrow and, when an amendment to the assize in 1405–6 required them to be made of the width of broadcloth, it was quickly withdrawn. In 1411 this obnoxious requirement was reimposed; two leading citizens went to London to remonstrate, but proved unsuccessful, and a demonstration of the impossibility of fulfilling the assize was attempted, by sending up cloths in the raw, partly fulled, and fully fulled and stretched. This also failed, and the law was not relaxed until 1433.

In 1421 a meeting to ventilate this and other grievances was attended by 81 master weavers, 207 weavers' workmen, 70 master fullers and 30 fullers' workmen, figures which suggest that 500 or more citizens were directly supported by clothmaking. Much of the cloth attributed to Salisbury names in the aulnage returns was in fact made outside the city, not only in its suburbs, but in an industrial hinterland which probably stretched through Wiltshire and north Somerset towards Bristol. Possibly it was just brought there to be sold, but equally it may have been made on behalf of merchants in the city. If so, this signified the emergence of the capitalist organiser – in these early days called draper or clothman, later clothier – who typically owned the materials from raw wool to finished cloth and organised workpeople, either under his own direct control or in their own homes, to convert the one to the other.

In Salisbury in the 15th century, however, some craftsmen owned and sold their own cloth, and since there was a part of the Market Place where yarn was sold, materials could change hands at an intermediate stage of manufacture. The weavers and fullers, both organised in guilds, included at least some men of property in their ranks. But the rewards of the industry were to go more and more to the clothiers, who arose in areas until now remote from the economics of manufacture and export.

The growing industry spread over considerable parts of two counties. In the 14th century there were more fulling mills in west Wiltshire – at Whaddon (from which two Trowbridge men stole cloth) in 1306, at Castle Combe in 1340, and at Bratton in 1348. Near Keevil, Baldham Mill had racks in 1372, and about the same time a Trowbridge man took a lease of part of the castle site in which to put a rack. In 1391 a Salisbury clothier complained of the way one of his cloths had been fulled at Westbury Leigh, some 25 miles away. A more general picture comes from the poll tax of 1379, though returns do not survive for all parts of the county. Small concentrations of clothworkers appear at a number of places as far apart as Christian Melford in the north, where there were 13 weavers and a fuller, and Mere in the south, where 13 fullers worked. In the Wylye valley especially, fullers appear in ones and twos at a number of villages in a way that suggests that there was a mill at each place. The manor of Frome included a fulling mill by 1349, and a survey of 1392 mentions pieces of land with racks on them, as well as five fulling mills. There was a mill at Twerton in 1324, and a street in Bath was called 'La Rekkestret' in 1333, and Chaucer's goodwife:

> 'Of cloth-makying she had swich an haunt,
> She passed them of Ypres and of Gaunt.'

She came from *biside* Bath, so that Chaucer and his audience knew of the celebrity of cloth making in the rural area around the city.

An unusually well-preserved group of manorial records pictures the cloth-making community of Castle Combe in the 15th century. Sir John Fastolf, lord of the manor, clothed his own troops in the French wars in his red and white livery, to the value of £100 a year, and the village became renowned for red dyeing. Red cloths called Castlecombes were the subject of a lawsuit in London in 1457, and some years earlier red cloths from the village were on sale at Blackwell Hall in London, already the centre of trade for English and foreign buyers. A description of the manor in 1454 distinguishes between Overcombe, where the husbandman lived, and Nethercombe, the centre for clothmaking; 50 new houses had been built during Fastolf's ownership. He would have gained, not only by increased rents and entry fines paid for his property, but also, in at least one instance, because a man who had made money out of the industry was still a villein of the manor.

ABOVE LEFT: Deed of a fulling mill at Stanley near Calne, early 13th century. (WRO) RIGHT & BELOW: Cloth seals found in the Avon at Bradford. (AP) CENTRE: Shears carved on Seend church. (SCP)

This was William Haynes, whose prosperity at his death in 1435 was so great that Fastolf's counsel said his goods were worth £2,000. A jury subsequently revised this to a net figure of £200, besides some debts, which included a payment of £20 towards the rebuilding of the church tower. Haynes's widow paid the lord £40 for possession of his goods, and subsequently another £100 for entry into his lands and permission to remarry. His property included a fulling mill and a gig-mill, the latter a machine for raising the nap on cloth, by setting the teazles in a revolving drum, over which the cloth was drawn in the reverse direction. Haynes's brother-in-law, Richard Halwey, occupied a fulling mill at Coleham, just outside the village. Clothiers such as these clearly employed numbers of weavers, dyers, and fullers, and in 1444 wardens for these crafts were appointed in the manorial court. Their office was probably no more than to attempt to prevent their members from misdemeanours such as tavern-haunting and poaching, and the industry itself flourished virtually unregulated, except for the assize under the control of the aulnager.

All over our area there rose from obscurity men like Haynes and Halwey, men who now proudly called themselves clothman, clothmaker, or clothier. Their business transactions only survive by chance, generally when they were in trouble with the law or in dispute among themselves. In 1420, for instance, John Draper of Trowbridge had two cloths, one coloured 'clover subtil', and the other frost green, detained by the aulnager at Bristol, and John Wykes of the same place had 102 white cloths arrested there in 1459 as not aulnaged. In the same year, Wykes sold 20 cloths worth £100 to Italian merchants in London, and William Adlam of Westbury 26 cloths worth £99 to German merchants, also in London. James Towker of Bradford sold 29 white cloths to a Venetian merchant at Bridport in 1463, and in 1468, when he had moved to Trowbridge, bought £40 worth of wool from the Hungerford family of Farleigh Hungerford. All the wool from the widespread Hungerford estates was brought for sale then to Farleigh, convenient for Bradford, Trowbridge and Frome.

More copious evidence of the prosperity of the clothmen comes from their wills, which reflect the mediaeval view, that even a man with a family should leave part of his worldly estate to pious uses. Sometimes this took the form of a gift to the church, such as the suit of vestments left to the church of Frome by Henry Dunkerton in 1419, or the silver-gilt cross given to St Michael's at Bath by William Philps in 1443. Philps also ordered his executors to finish a chapel of St Katharine, which he had begun; the chapel was perhaps associated with the Fraternity of St Katharine, to which Thomas Chaunceler left two looms in 1496.

Clothmen are known to have contributed towards the rebuilding of several churches, and so many in this area were rebuilt or improved then that there must have been many gifts of which we know nothing. At Trowbridge, John Wykes left £10 in 1460, the great furnace of his dyehouse, and 13 oak trees to the new works in the church there and, towards the end of the century, John Stokes added a new north aisle at Seend, causing it to be marked with a pair of clothier's shears on the outside. About 1515 Keevil church received legacies from two clothiers; one of them, Walter Lucas of Steeple Ashton, paid for the south aisle in his own village, and a fellow clothier, Robert Long, provided the north aisle. The church, largely rebuilt between 1480 and 1500, is the finest monument to this prosperous period and curiously, was built to the design of Thomas Lovell of Trowbridge, variously described as a freemason and a clothman. At his death in 1505 he too left money to Ashton church, and to the building of the market cross at Trowbridge.

Such benefactions were held to be for the health of the dead man's soul. Many clothiers, however, took more specific steps to ensure that they would be comfortable after death. William Philps, for instance, made his gift of a cross conditional on his name being included with those of other benefactors to be specially commended, and also left money to provide a priest to celebrate masses for his soul for seven years. Thomas Chaunceler of Bath arranged for a priest for twenty years, and laid down details of elaborate funeral celebrations, which were to last for 30 days. The most prosperous (or most pious) endowed permanent chantries, of which the best documented is that at Trowbridge; founded by James Towker, under his *alias* of Terumber, it was endowed with property in the town (including Terumber's own house), and at Bradford, Beckington, and Broughton Gifford, the rents of which paid the stipend of a priest, and for the upkeep of an almshouse for six poor people. The names of Terumber's trustees in the foundation deed show that he was able to enlist many of the local gentry to act on his behalf.

Other clothmen clearly invested in valuables, and many wills refer to particular pieces of silver plate, as well as considerable sums of money left to wives and children. Lands could also be purchased, either freehold or more frequently, copyhold or leasehold. Fulling mills were naturally sought after. Wiliam Sewey, clothman, in 1458 was able to buy a 96 – year lease of a large fulling mill, with four pairs of stocks, at Stowford near Farleigh Hungerford, and lived on the site, so that he was frequently known as William Stowford. But not all clothmen made mills their headquarters. John Wykes lived in the town at Trowbridge rather than at his mill just outside the town, and Lawrence Stephens of Keevil (d 1486) lived on the site of the present Blagden House, rather than at his mill of Bulkington, at the end of a long lane to the south.

The mills may simply have been run by the owners' workpeople, or may have been let to specialist fullers, who then took in work from a number of clothmen, charging them by the cloth. More mills were used for fulling in the 15th century: at Littleton (near Semington), Market Lavington, Penleigh (near Westbury), and a notable group on the Wylye just below Warminster, where five stood on a five-mile stretch between that town and Boyton. One of these, at Heytesbury, was built by the Hungerford family in 1421–2. Further downstream, one of the smaller Langford villages was called 'Tokynglangford' in 1435. Investment was certainly not limited to mills but included house building at Castle Combe; at Mells in the late 15th century, Abbot Selwood of Glastonbury, impressed by the prosperity of the cloth industry, built a street of houses which still stand near the church.

Bequests such as that by Thomas Chaunceler of Bath in 1496, of 12d each to all his weavers and tuckers throughout the town, indicate that the putting out system was already established. Chaunceler also left three looms for charitable purposes; one was to be used for life by his brother-in-law. Other wills mention apprentices and journeymen, so some clothiers probably had workpeople in house as well as piece workers outside.

Much coloured cloth was made throughout the clothing district in the 15th century; Salisbury was a centre for the distribution of dyestuffs such as woad and madder, and of alum, used as a mordant, imported through Southampton. Woad especially was a much-valued commodity, so that clothiers left it in their wills; Simon Lacy of Leigh-on-Mendip left a pipe of woad, and a woad vat, furnace, and lead cistern with pipes, to the church there in 1482, and bequests of woad in the area between Wells and Bath are sufficiently frequent to suggest that it specialised in blue cloth. Bruton russets were well-known by 1440. References to dyehouses also come from Wiltshire, where John Wykes had one at Trowbridge in 1460, and John Gatford at the same place in 1497. Gatford had a workshop with shears, an indication that the coloured cloths were also finished locally. In Salisbury, too, references to fullers, tuckers, and shearmen (all synonymous terms for finishers of cloth), and to the shears, teazles, and presses they worked with, suggest the same.

Nevertheless, there was also an extensive export trade in white broadcloth, exported after fulling but before dyeing, raising or shearing. As early as 1429, white cloth, 'western blankett of the Vyze [Devizes] and Bekenton', was being sold to foreigners, and the cloths called bastards being exported through Southampton in the 1470s were apparently white. In 1477–8 almost 400 came from two Devizes clothiers: over 200 from John Horton of Westwood, and 40 from William Stowford. But by then London was the chief focus of this export. Cloth taken there was sold to merchants for re-sale in the low countries and in Italy, to be finished in cities, which had once been famous manufacturing centres. References to this trade almost all come from west Wiltshire and the valley of the Frome. By 1500 this trade appears to have become the most valuable, and the area the most prosperous, in our region.

21

ABOVE: The Market Cross, Castle Combe, BELOW: Steeple Ashton
church.

Golden Age

A good picture of the location of the white broadcloth trade comes from the surviving account book of a London merchant, Thomas Kitson, which runs from 1529 to 1540. Kitson bought mainly from an area best defined as the valley of the Bristol Avon and its tributaries, from Malmesbury down to Bath, and that of the Wylye as far south as Heytesbury. Outlying suppliers were at Bristol and Keynsham to the north-west, and at Wilton and Salisbury to the south. Noticeably absent from his book are the valley of the By Brook, in which Castle Combe stands, and the western fringes running from Bruton to Pensford, areas in which we know that coloured cloths were made.

This was also true of Salisbury, where comparatively light-weight coloured cloths called kerseys were important. The same trade flourished briefly in the Kennet valley, mainly at Newbury, where Jack of Newbury (John Winchcombe) was to become a legendary figure, and this brought a brief return of the industry to the Marlborough area. Salisbury stood apart from the main industrial area, not only geographically, but also in organisation. The actual clothmaking was often still carried out by independent craftsmen; weavers bought their yarn in the market, and may well have sold their cloths straight from the loom to one of the many independent fullers, to be milled and finished; clothiers were hardly distinguished from weavers in prosperity. Cloths were not sent up to London, but sold locally to Salisbury merchants who carried on trade through Southampton, exporting cloth and wool, and importing a wide range of goods including dyestuffs and the olive oil which was used to oil the wool before carding. But Salisbury was overshadowed, though by no means eclipsed, as a textile centre, by the white broadcloth area.

Another account book which survives is that of John Smythe, merchant of Bristol, kept between 1538 and 1550. His trade was comparable to that of the Salisbury merchants, exporting cloth as well as leather, corn and lead, and importing wine, iron, dyestuffs and oil. Smythe exported almost entirely coloured cloth; some came from Suffolk, Wales and the north, but his main suppliers were from the western parts of the Somerset clothing area. From clothiers such as John Yerbury of Bruton, Thomas Ashe of Batcombe, William Butcher of Coley, and James Bisse of Stoke Lane, he bought cloths of a middle price range called 'penny hewes', and cheap cloths called truckers. Other descriptions indicate particular colours such as 'azars' (azures), 'plonkettes' (greys), and 'sadblewes' or 'sadgrenes'. A good deal of the cloth was brought to Bristol unfinished, Smythe employing Bristol tuckers and shearmen to dress them, and occasionally dyers to change the colours. His cloth exports went mainly to Gascony and Spain. Smythe imported and sold large quantities of woad, both to his own clothiers and to others, mainly in the same area. Most came from Toulouse or from the Azores. Olive oil was also imported in great quantities.

When John Leland, the King's antiquary, came here in about 1540 he passed through this western section of the clothing district. Pensford, 'a praty market townlet occupied with clothing', Wells, where one Mawdelyne had been a great clothier and had been succeeded by his son, and Bruton, were all mentioned as flourishing places, but of Chew Magna and Mells, Leland used the past tense, as though the trade had fallen away. Bath he also considered 'sumwhat decayed' owing to the deaths of three recent clothiers, Style, Kent and Chapman. Elsewhere, however, he remarked on the opulent buildings, 'fayre stone housys' at Frome, and at 'a botome' two miles from it (probably Spring Gardens): a 'pratie stone house' and 'a goodly large chirche house' built by one Horton at Bradford: 'dyvers fair howsys' also built by Horton at Trowbridge, a town 'very welle buildid of stone'; and 'praty buyldinge' at Steeple Ashton. All these he described as important cloth-making centres, as he did also Devizes, Westbury, and Norton St Philip.

The Horton mentioned at Bradford was Thomas, son of John Horton, clothmaker, who died in 1497 at Iford on the River Frome, where he must have had the fulling mill. Thomas settled at Bradford, where he acquired another fulling mill, still keeping the Iford one. His profits were invested in a widespread property, which included the manor house at Westwood, which he remodelled, leaving his initials on a chimney piece there and on the tower of the nearby church. He died at Westwood in 1530, but was buried at Bradford, where he and his wife are to be seen on a brass. He endowed a chantry and school in the church, leaving the remainder of his property to a nephew and namesake. This younger Thomas was assessed at £10 in the taxation of 1545 – a sum exceeded by only one taxpayer (a Salisbury merchant) in the county. He left two sons who carried on his business, and daughters who married into other clothing families – the Baileys and Yerburys of Trowbridge, the Longs of Whaddon, and the Winchcombes of Newbury. By the end of the century the Hortons were gentry, and some idea of their prosperity may be gained from the probate inventory of Edward Horton, who retired to Bath and died in 1603 worth £22,000.

At Trowbridge Leland mentioned two clothiers – 'old Bayllie' and 'one Alexandre'. The former, who had built much property in the town according to Leland, was Thomas Bailey, who died in 1543. 'Bailies sun now drapeth yn the toune and also a 2 miles out of it at a place yn the way to Farley-Castel': this was Christopher Bailey and his mill at Stowford, where his house may still be seen, adjoining a later mill. 'Alexandre' was Alexander Langford who died in 1545, making provision for masses to be said for him for two years, and for widespread benefactions to the poor. They both left extensive properties; besides Christopher, Bailey had sons in the trade at Baldham Mill near Keevil and at Devizes, both heavily assessed in 1545, though not equalling two other Trowbridge clothiers. These were Anthony Passion and Thomas Long, most prosperous after Thomas Horton. Passion mainly traded from Littleton Mill near Semington. Long died in 1562, still active although lord of nine manors, which passed to his nephew Edward Long and became the foundation of the landed estate of the Longs of Rood Ashton.

A fourth Wiltshire clothier mentioned by Leland was William Stumpe of Malmesbury. Stumpe had just bought all the domestic buildings of the abbey for over £1,500: 'every corner of the vaste offices that belongid to thabbay be fulle of lumbes to weve cloth yn, and this Stumpe entendith to make a stret or 2 for clothiers in the bak vacant ground of the abbay'. The latter apparently came to nothing, as did an agreement to buy other monastic buildings at Oseney in Oxfordshire, and we do not know how long Stumpe's weavers worked together at Malmesbury. Weavers preferred to work at home, though shop conditions prevented embezzlement of materials, a regular source of complaint in the future. Stumpe sat in Parliament for Malmesbury, served as sheriff of Wiltshire, and was a justice of the peace in Wiltshire and Gloucestershire. When he died in 1552 his son James had already been knighted. William Stumpe's property eventually passed to three great-granddaughters, who married the Earls of Suffolk, Lincoln, and Rutland.

The industry which Leland described was probably then at its zenith. The export of English cloth, especially that of broadcloth sent to the continent through London, had risen dramatically since 1500, and by 1550 the production of white broadcloth overshadowed all else. Salisbury's export of coloured cloths through Southampton decayed after 1550 and, twenty years later, the only Salisbury merchant trading through that port was dealing mainly in Hampshire cloth. He went bankrupt in 1577. But Salisbury offered too many advantages as a textile centre for manufacture to end and, by the early part of Elizabeth's reign, much white broadcloth from the city was sold in London. This trade may well have been promoted by clothiers moving in, like Thomas Whelpley (a former mayor of Bath) and John Compton of Beckington, while the first known clothier Mayor of Salisbury was John Bailey (1577), of a family well-known in west Wiltshire.

The region south of Bristol, which exported coloured cloth through that port, probably suffered a similar decay, the industry disappearing entirely from its western parts by the end of the 16th century.

The second half of the century was more difficult for cloth exporters. In the fifties and sixties the religious wars on the continent, and especially the fall of Antwerp, disrupted trade, the Spanish war from 1586 likewise. Periods of depression were apt to alarm the government, and focussed its attention on complaints about the poor quality of cloth produced. The check on size formerly carried out by the aulnagers had become a dead letter, though the aulnagers still sold seals to the clothiers, and the proceeds went to the Crown. It was indeed possible for a mill owner to seal cloths. John Clevelode of Beckington in 1537 left a fulling mill with cloth seal called 'le oynage', *ie* aulnage, and Jeffrey Whitaker of Tinhead left the benefit of the seal of three mills in 1601.

Westwood Manor, by W.W. Wheatley c1850. (DM)

In 1550 the size and weight of properly-made broadcloths were laid down by statute, and the appointment of overseers of cloth by the justices was ordered. Other acts were intended to stimulate cloth making in corporate towns at the expense of the country clothier, to encourage apprenticeship, and to prohibit the use of the gig-mill in raising the nap on cloth.

Some of these regulations quickly fell into abeyance, for the country clothiers were too powerful to be brought to heel by London merchants. But the fact that all cloths sent to London had to be sold at Blackwell Hall gave the merchants an initial advantage. In 1559–60 they managed to circumvent a statutory provision that cloth searched in the country was exempt from further search in London, and cloths brought to the hall were checked, often by plunging them into water, to see if they had been over-stretched on the tenter racks and so rendered faulty. Clothiers who brought faulty cloths were fined. After a few years the zeal of the Blackwell Hall searchers abated, but it was not until 1589–91 that a group of clothiers, by taking the London searchers to law, established a right of exemption. Even so, the alleged practice of over-stretching, and the difference between dry and wet measure, remained a constant source of bad blood between producers and merchants.

A similar victory was obtained by the country clothiers (who included those living in non-corporate towns such as Trowbridge, Bradford, and Frome) over legislation designed to limit the scale of clothmaking. It was gained after a series of prosecutions of prominent clothiers brought by a mischievous Frome clothier, Peter Blackborrow, in 1575. Regulation by enforcing apprenticeships, especially to weaving, was more successful, and regularly enforced by the justices, who also laid down detailed wage rates. The Wiltshire justices, and probably those in Somerset, reinforced the examination of cloths by appointed searchers and prosecutions for short, light or over-stretched cloths, were frequent in the early 17th century.

In spite of regulation, or perhaps because of it, the industry slowly recovered from the setbacks of the earlier part of Elizabeth's reign, and by 1600 exports, mainly to Holland and Germany, had probably regained mid-century levels. The product was still largely white unfinished broadcloth, sent up to London for sale to merchants, who either exported it unfinished or had it dyed and finished in London. Only occasionally was coloured cloth from our area seen at Blackwell Hall, as when reds from Keevil and plunkets from Westubury were reported faulty there in 1574–5. But reference to dyers, often men of some prosperity, and to clothiers who owned shears, are sufficiently frequent to show that a proportion of cloth was finished locally, and probably sold at fairs in Salisbury and Bristol.

The second half of the 16th century provides many examples of how two or three generations of a clothing family would make enough money to invest in land, and infiltrate the gentry. In the 1565 Herald's visitation of Wiltshire, we find the Alleynes of Calne, Baileys of Trowbridge, Bennetts of Norton Bavant, Burleys and Flowers of Potterne, Hortons of Westwood, Mays of Broughton Gifford, and Michells of Calstone. The Horton involvement in trade ended in the early 17th century, as did that of the Yerburys of Trowbridge and the Longs of Whaddon. Other families on the way up were the Whitakers of Tinhead, whose house (now called Becketts) still stands, and the Topps and Potticarys of Stockton. Inevitably we know less of the smaller clothiers, who certainly existed; they bought wool in local markets, often in quantities so small that they could not be properly mixed, or else badly-spun yarn – at least according to the larger clothiers, who attempted from time to time to curtail the activities of the wool broggers and yarn jobbers which, they said, led to the making of faulty cloth.

Such condemnation often arose from the conventional dislike of the middleman, inherited from mediaeval times, and there is plenty of evidence that large clothiers also bought wool at markets at Cirencester, Tetbury, Castle Combe, and Devizes. The most costly came from the Welsh border, conventionally called Leominster wool, and from the Cotswolds, where the large clothiers would also make direct purchases from the wool growers. Christopher Pyard of Trowbridge died at Northampton in 1521; in his hurried will he left a cow to a friend at home, for explaining to his wife about the parcels of wool and how to gather them in. A good deal was also bought in the clothing district itself, and many clothiers of the richer sort were farmers, like John Flower of Potterne, who owned 800 sheep in Henry VIII's reign.

John Irish, a maker of the blue broadcloth at Yatton before 1578, used his house to 'break his woolle, oyle and sorte the same, and put the same to spynnynge, tuckinge, and weavinge from his said howse'. His wool was dyed by specialist dyers until he was able to build a dyehouse of his own. Weavers were sometimes prosperous, owning several looms, and often farming stock. But the majority were poor, often only renting the looms they worked on, and frequently living in cottages of the meanest kind erected on the fringes of waste lands, so widespread locally in pre-enclosure times. A survey of Steeple Ashton manor in 1637 lists 138 such cottages on the wastes in and around that village, North Bradley and Southwick. They already had a reputation for turbulent and riotous behaviour.

When the clothier received the cloth back from his weaver it went to the fulling mill to be brayed and then fulled. Well over 60 mills, stretching from Malmesbury to Salisbury, and westward to

ABOVE: Talboys House, Keevil, home of the clothier Thomas Barkesdale;
BELOW: West Lavington, fulling mill to left with later clothier's house.

27

Pensford and Bruton, were in use in the 16th century. In the valley of the Bristol Avon, most were on the tributaries, which were easier to control with hatches and weirs. The massive weir still to be seen at Avoncliff, just below Bradford, may date back to 1590, when the place was known as Ancles Weers. Other mills on the main stream were at Melksham, Staverton, Bradford, Limpley Stoke, and Twerton. On the seven-mile River Marden were seven mills; on the Semington Brook and tributaries, six, and on the River Biss, five. The River Frome was particularly favoured: between Frome and its mouth were mills at Spring Gardens, Lullington, Clifford, Shawford, Rode, Langham, Tellisford, Stowford, Farleigh, Iford, and Freshford.

Many mills were held on lease by the principal clothing families. Trowbridge families, for instance, held at different times in the 16th century the mills at Stowford (Bailey), Tellisford (Wallis), Freshford (Langford), Rode (Pyard), Littleton (Passion), Bulkington (Bailey), Langham (Passion), and Clifford (Langford). Some clothiers lived at their mills. Geoffrey Hawkins 'planted himself in the art of clothing' at the mill at Norton Bavant c1570, and other notable examples were the Chivers of Quemerford near Calne and the Wilkinses of Brook near Westbury. But if clothiers chose, as most apparently did, to live in market towns or the larger villages, they could have the mills run on their behalf. Families were large and a younger brother might occupy a mill: rich Trowbridge clothier Thomas Wallis had a brother Thomas at the mill in 1558. Mills could also be underlet to specialised fullers, who then took work on commission from their landlords and from other clothiers. In 1584 Henry Long of Whaddon, a rich clothier, charged 2s 8d for milling a medium-grade cloth, and 1s 8d for a coarse one. On the whole, it seems likely that specialised fullers worked many of the mills.

If cloths were finished locally, those processes were sometimes done at the mill too. Bitham Mill at Westbury had a loft 'with all things fitting for the dressing of cloth' in 1573. Other clothiers may have had the work done at home by their own people, or put it out on commission. The use of gig mills for raising the nap on the cloth was forbidden by statute in 1552, and seems to have dropped out of use after a few prosecutions. It was probably never in wide use in an area which concentrated on unfinished cloth.

The clothier's final task was to do up the cloths in packs of ten and send them by carrier to London, to be sold in Blackwell Hall in Basinghall Street, rebuilt in 1588. Some large clothiers employed factors there; others travelled up with their own consignments and those of neighbours. Sales in the hall were made direct to drapers or mercers for home consumption, or to Merchant Adventurers for export. Sales also took place to Hansard merchants, who obtained direct access to Blackwell Hall at the end of the 15th century. The surviving account books of Mathias Hoep, a Hamburg merchant (1566–72) show that he bought extensively from Thomas Long and Robert Wallis of Trowbridge. But their presence in the hall caused resentment, and their privileges were curtailed little by little. The final closure of their headquarters in the Steelyard in 1598 left the Merchant Adventurers with a virtual monopoly of the trade to the Netherlands and Germany.

The price made by cloths depended, not only on the visible quality, but on the reputation of the maker, attested by his mark. It was important to maintain the reputation of a mark (hence our phrase 'up to the mark') and, when William Blagden of Trowbridge left his wife his green cloth mark for life, he provided that, if she remarried, her husband was to become bound to the overseers of his will 'to keep the cloth in the same goodness as at my death', so that it would pass uninjured to Blagden's son. Thomas Long of Trowbridge had a cloth mark called 'the red world' in 1562, probably the same one his widow left to her nephew William Yerbury in 1583. Marks were frequently left in wills, as when Nash Whitaker of Tinhead left his 'best cloth mark called the Yellow Cross with N and W thereunto annexed' in 1598. They varied with quality, either by different colours, or designs, as the 'red castle' and 'golden ball' both used by Robert Ray of Salisbury c1600. Marks could be sold too, and the £20 William Wilkins of Trowbridge received for his shows the value of a good one.

ABOVE: Stowford House. BELOW: Mark of Edward Cogswell on a
fireplace at Westbury Leigh, 1591.

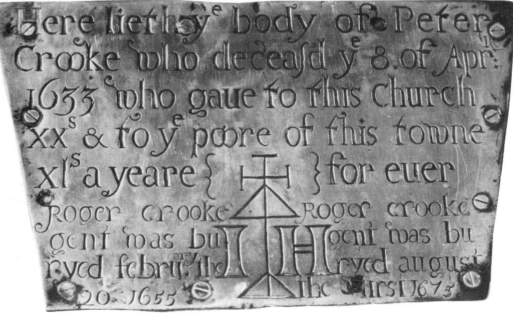

ABOVE: Mark of Joseph Martyn, Trowbridge, 1622, (WRO) and BELOW:
of Peter Crooke, Steeple Ashton, 1633.

Spanish Wool & Dutchmen

The early years of the 17th century were comparatively prosperous. White broadcloth for export dominated the district, and 60 per cent of that exported came from our area, with most of the balance from Gloucestershire and the city of Worcester. Other types of cloth were made here too: cheaper fabrics, of the type then called 'new draperies'. They were often made with a worsted warp and a woollen weft, but finished like cloth, and formed the principal product of the East Anglian and northern textile industries. In the west they were probably made by the smaller clothiers, and in quantity were unimportant compared with the broadcloth.

On this long-established and prosperous, though static, industry fell in 1614 a blow from an unexpected quarter. James I, persuaded by a group of merchants led by Alderman Sir William Cockayne of London, withdrew the privileges of the Merchant Adventurers and transferred them to a new company, which undertook to export all the available broadcloth, after it had been finished in London. The Dutch immediately forbade the import of all English cloth, other markets could not be found, and Alderman Cockayne's project, as it has ever since been called, collapsed within two years. The old Merchant Adventurers were restored, and exports resumed, but merchants and clothiers had suffered losses, and distress was widespread among the workpeople. Then the disruption caused in Germany by the Thirty Years' War began to affect trade. Meanwhile competition from new draperies produced elsewhere in England, and from rising textile industries in France and Holland, were also having their effects. By 1640 the export of white broadcloth had been halved since 1600, and it continued to decline intermittently, finally petering out in the early 18th century.

The centre of the white broadcloth industry had been in west Wiltshire and the parts of Somerset immediately adjoining, extending probably to include Frome, where several clothing families of status, not far short of the greatest in Trowbridge and Bradford, had flourished in Elizabeth's reign. But the parts further west, around Shepton Mallet and beyond, seem to have gone on making that coloured cloth produced there in the time of Henry VIII. The regulating act of 1552 laid down the size and weight of reds, broad plunkets, azures, and blues made in Somerset. Late in the century some clothiers of Shepton Mallet were making light blue cloth for export to Holland and Germany, where it was dyed again and worn by the 'better sort of people'. A bill was proposed in 1606, to prevent the export of this cloth unfinished; the petitions show that they were dyed violet, purple, or green abroad. After Cockayne's project, the export of such cloths, then said to be made in Wiltshire and Somerset, was apparently resumed.

It may have been from this sector of the trade, smaller in scale than the white broadcloth and occupying much less attention on the national stage, that the product emerged which was to be the salvation of the western industry. It was called Spanish cloth. The credit for its introduction was claimed (and the claim was believed by informed contemporaries) by Benedict Webb, a native of Beckington who had been apprenticed to a London mercer and sent by his master to France. In the late 1580s Webb began to make at Taunton 'a sort of medley cloth which Mr. William Stone, a mercer in Cheapside dealt with me for, and cald them Spanish Clothes'. The name medley, often used for these cloths as well, describes the method of mixing wool dyed of various colours in differing proportions before carding and spinning, so that a wide range of colours could be produced. This may not have been a complete innovation, but a substantial improvement. Using fine wool (mainly, though not entirely, imported from Spain) makers were able to produce a high-quality cloth, considerably lighter in weight than anything of comparable finish previously made.

Apart from Webb's activities, which by 1600 were carried out from Kingswood in Gloucestershire, the early development of the Spanish cloth manufacture is obscure. A pamphlet called *The Young Man's Looking Glass* published in 1641 implies that several clothiers in and near Shepton Mallet had made fortunes by it. One of these was James Ashe of Westcombe in Batcombe parish. His son John married a daughter of Henry Davison, a Freshford clothier, and began to make Spanish cloth there in the 1620s. There was also an increase in activity by market spinners. This inevitably produced loud complaints from clothiers still in the white cloth trade, who believed that at least some of the yarn was made from wool pilfered by their spinners, who then added grease and dirt to make up the weight of wool they had been given. A bitter dispute arose in the 1630s, largely centreing around Anthony Wither, a government commissioner investigating the observance of clothing laws in the west. Wither sided with the white clothiers and, when the commission reported, their suppression was one proposal designed to enforce stricter regulation. But the report was made in 1640, too late for action.

The growing market for Spanish cloths led some to imitate them, by dyeing cloths of English wool 'in the say', *ie* straight after weaving and before fulling. In 1630 and 1634 makers of Spanish cloth and Merchant Adventurers petitioned the government against this, on the grounds that it was inferior and would discount Spanish cloth. Two leading say-dyed clothiers, William Brewer of Lullington and Christopher Brewer of Beckington, were examined before the Privy Council. Finally, in 1640, the Council ordered the say-dyed clothiers to weave a distinctive list into their cloths, to show how they were made, and to use special marks. They commented approvingly on the quality of their dyeing, some being as good or better than that of the Dutch, but nevertheless forbade the export of their cloths to the markets of the Merchant Adventurers, only allowing them to go to the Baltic and the Mediterranean. It is curious that no more is heard of this apparently-promising trade after the Civil War.

The Civil War had no far-reaching effect on the new direction that the industry was taking, though it probably delayed the full effects of change. The majority of clothiers whose sympathies are known were for Parliament, and some, like John Ashe of Freshford and William Strode of Shepton Mallet, took an active role. Local leadership for the King's party came more typically from the families which had given up trade for a generation or two, as at Trowbridge where Edward Yerbury and Henry Wallis were active while the town was in the hands of Royalist troops. Passage to London was difficult from time to time, but the Merchant Adventurers were protected by Parliament, and exports both of white and medley cloths continued. By the 1650s, however, Dutch duties on English cloth had increased to a degree that concentrated the company's trade more and more at Hamburg, and by the end of the century it was known as the Hamburg Company.

By the Restoration it is clear that Spanish cloth formed the most important sector of the trade. The process of change had been accompanied by some complaints of depression and distress, and the industry seems to have receded entirely from some places, at least insofar as they were no longer the headquarters of clothiers. Little more is heard, for instance, of Malmesbury, and the previously-important villages of Edington, Bratton, and Steeple Ashton were from now on no more than the dwelling-places of weavers and their families. To the west the trade became unimportant, though not quite extinct, in the villages in the Chew valley. In other places the vacuum left by the decline of white clothmaking was filled by fabrics other than Spanish cloth. Devizes and Calne in particular were noted for serges, which had a worsted warp and a woollen weft, while druggets, a narrow material also with a worsted warp which could be finished like fine cloth, were made all over the area. Salisbury began to make flannel about 1680, though its staple product remained white cloth, dyed in London, and exported by the Levant company.

The 'new draperies' made partly of worsted were cheaper than Spanish cloth, and were probably made by clothiers of less wealth. The larger clothiers, turning more and more to Spanish cloth, were at first confronted with the difficulty of spinning the very short and soft Spanish wool into yarn strong enough for the warp, and it is likely that at first English wool was used for this. In Holland, however, it was known that this difficulty had been overcome, and fine Dutch cloth was imported into England until a heavy duty was imposed to keep it out. In 1674 it was outselling English cloth in eastern Europe because of the superior quality of Dutch spinning, dyeing and finishing.

Selwood Road, Frome

Until this time, immigrant 'Flemish weavers', so firmly entrenched in local folklore, are absent from reliable sources, and foreign influence on the industry had been negligible. About 1657, however, Paul Methuen of Bradford (son-in-law of John Ashe) brought over a Dutch spinner, and within a short time is known to have been using Spanish wool in large quantities. Aubrey spoke of Methuen as the greatest clothier of his time; he died in 1666, and Aubrey said rather later that William Brewer of Trowbridge 'drove the greatest trade for medleys of any clothier in England'. In 1672 a Royal proclamation inviting Dutch artisans to settle in England led to the arrival of 23 Dutchmen 'skilled in the art of making fine cloth' in 1673. They, and another 10 in 1674, were sent down to Brewer at Trowbridge, where he settled some in a house he owned in Polebarn Lane. Three, described rather vaguely as 'Dutchmen by nation or of Poland' were sent to Bradford, where the name of Dutch Barton still belongs to a group of houses, and others may have gone to neighbouring towns.

There is no doubt that the Dutch brought several improved techniques, quickly adopted. Among them were changes in the preparation of wool before spinning, so that it involved two processes. The first of these, called scribbling, was carried out in the clothier's own workshop by repeatedly drawing the wool with hand cards over a scribbling horse, a frame covered with iron teeth set in leather leaves. The word scribble is derived from the German *schrubbel* and the earliest use of it so far found dates from 1675. The scribbling process differed significantly from the preliminary stock-carding done on a bench, referred to as early as 1615 as necessary for medleys, and that the Dutch no doubt brought it. Once the spinners had the scribbled wool, they carded it on hand cards, and here again the Dutch brought improvement in the form of superior cards. In the late 17th century Frome was the most important card-making centre in England, and it was said in 1709 that the import of foreign cards and the wire to make them had stopped since the arrival of the Dutch. They may have brought other improvements, for Dutch spinning was mentioned at Trowbridge in 1706, and Brewer owned Dutch looms at his death a year later. Dutch finishing was much admired at the time, and better techniques were probably introduced in that field too.

By the 1680s it seems that Spanish cloth had improved in quality and at the same time become cheaper. Improved spinning, John Aubrey was told, meant that a pound of wool made twice as much cloth as before the Civil War, so that cloth became lighter. The better qualities were now made entirely of Spanish wool, and became popular in the home market, especially after Charles II began to wear Spanish cloth in 1675. Comparatively little was exported, not because demand in France and Flanders was small, but because hostile tariffs made it too expensive. By 1704 it was said that total production of Spanish cloth was 30,000 pieces a year; much of this must have been made in Wiltshire and Somerset, for Gloucestershire and Worcester city, the other areas producing fine cloth, were concentrating on piece-dyed cloths, a good deal of which went to the Levant. Some Wiltshire cloth also went to this increasingly-important market, mainly from Salisbury.

Virtually no business records survive from before 1700. But we can be in no doubt about the prosperity of the principal clothiers. Families such as the Methuens of Bradford, the Brewers, Houltons and Coopers of Trowbridge, the Selfes and Awdrys of Melksham, the Scotts and Goldneys of Chippenham, the Jessers and Smiths of Frome, and the Strodes of Shepton Mallet, were pushing up into the landed gentry, as their predecessors had before them, making marriages which brought them more land and cash, sometimes with daughters of gentry, and sometimes of clothiers, serving as justices and high sheriffs, and acquiring coats of arms and sham pedigrees. In spite of this, many were Whigs and nonconformists, principal supporters of the chapels which were being licensed in the towns after the Toleration Act. Many congregations began to meet in workshops behind clothier's houses, and only built chapels at a later time; this is why chapels frequently stand behind the street line, approached only by a passage, as can be seen, for instance, in St Margaret's Street at Bradford.

Clothiers of the first rank probably concentrated on making cloth of the highest quality entirely from Spanish wool. Below them were a wide range of lesser men, such as George Wansey of Warminster, whose account books of 1683–1714 survive. He used mostly English wool, which he bought mainly in Warminster market, though some came from as far as Sussex. Spanish wool he had sent down from London to mix for his best cloths, those of the orange mark. He made up to ten cloths a week in the usual way, mainly by putting out, but he did his own dyeing and dressing. Besides cloth, he made some druggets and serges with worsted yarn bought for the warps. Wansey's affairs prospered sufficiently for him to build a house, buy leasehold property, and leave his wife £800 and a business still in the family a century later.

Another book to survive is that of William Gaby of Netherstreet in Bromham, who entered only random jottings, running from 1656 to 1684. He sold some cloth in London, and perhaps more locally, but many of his dealings were in yarn, and his farming was clearly at least as important as his clothing. In prosperity he may not have been different to the better-off among the workpeople, for wills and probate inventories (only available for Wiltshire) show that weavers and clothworkers could own small properties, farm stock, and household goods of some value. But those of whom we know were exceptional, and most workpeople were certainly poor enough.

Sheppard's Barton, Frome.

Another measure of the prosperity of the Spanish cloth manufacture comes from the towns themselves. By 1700 Bradford, Trowbridge, and Frome were established as the three leading centres for the making of the best cloth, and all had grown significantly in the past 40 years. At Bradford the terraces on the hillside above the old town were built up to an extent which led to the area being called Newtown as early as 1665; later 17th century dates can still be seen on several houses, and leases of plots of that period were made by the Methuen family. Trowbridge has retained much less, but two areas were built at this time – a group of several terraces known collectively as the Conigre, mainly on Houlton property, and Duke Street. But the most important expansion occurred at Frome.

When Defoe came to Frome soon after 1720, he compared the recent growth of the town with that of Manchester; 'they have built a new church, and so many new streets of houses, and those houses are so full of inhabitants, that Frome is now reckoned to have more people in it, than the city of Bath. . .and if their trade continues to increase. . .it is very likely to be one of the greatest and wealthiest inland towns of England'. However, soon after he wrote, the increase slackened, and the area in which most of the new houses were built remained largely intact and in use, though many houses had been altered by the fitting of new windows and addition of storeys in the 19th century.

In 1975 development threatened what had become known as the Trinity area (after a later church) and only in the nick of time was it realised that this group of streets represented the growth spoken of by Defoe. Careful documentary research and structural investigation has since revealed the detailed history of the area, from the building of the earliest houses soon after 1660, to the completion of the street plan by 1725. A large part of it has been saved and is now being rehabilitated, pronounced to be 'one of the earliest surviving planned urban developments for a semi-industrial population in England'.

For Bradford and Trowbridge there is also evidence from incomplete poor-law settlement certificates, of people moving in. In Bradford between 1673 and 1679 immigrants included 52 clothworkers, 19 weavers, and 10 other textile workers, while to Trowbridge between 1668 and 1679 came 25 clothworkers, seven weavers, and 10 scribblers. Almost all came from the Wiltshire and Somerset clothmaking area or from Gloucestershire. The way the industry was receding from the more western parts of Somerset is shown by immigrants from East Harptree, Pensford, Chew Magna and Queen Camel. But those who were able to bring certificates from their parishes were probably a minority. Between June 1676 and May 1679, the overseers of Trowbridge obtained from the justices the power to remove 220 men and 14 women, all adults, from the town. It must have been some industrial upsurge that brought people flocking in this way, and it is difficult not to connect it with the Dutch. It is also noteworthy that, of ten scribblers who turned up in Trowbridge in 1675–1677, seven came from Westbury. Could a Dutch scribbler have been sent there?

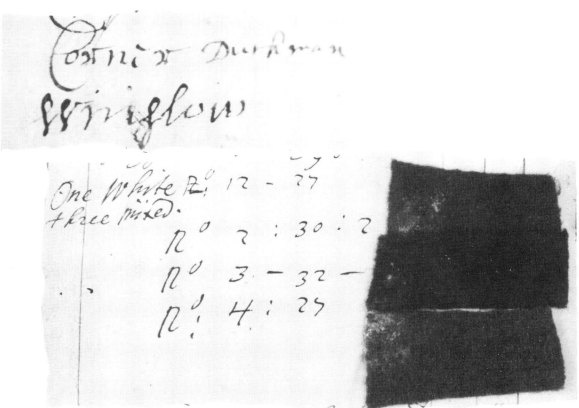

LEFT: Burial of 'Corner, Duchman', Trowbridge, 1692. (WRO) RIGHT: Patterns of druggets, George Wansey of Warminster, 1694. (WRO)

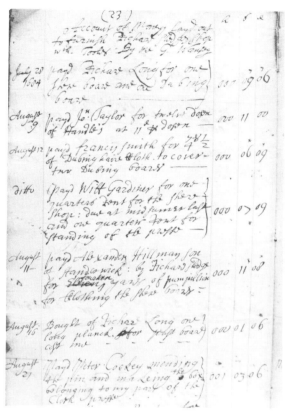

LEFT: George Wansey's expenditure in setting up a finishing shop, Warminster, 1684. (WRO) RIGHT: Newtown, Bradford, houses dated 1697. BELOW: Shepton Mallet, 17th-century houses.

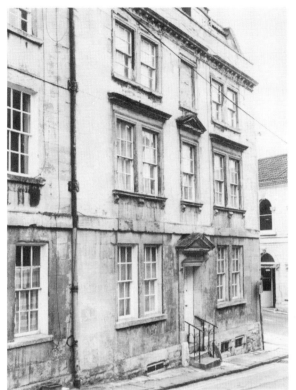

LEFT: Clothier's houses: Whitehead's Lane, Bradford; RIGHT: Greystone House, Devizes, the home of Stephen Hillman, whose account books survive; BELOW: Hilperton House.

Rich Man, Poor Man

The first 20 years of the 18th century saw the industry at its most prosperous since the introduction of Spanish cloth. From it the middle and upper classes, and their servants, were clothed, and it supplied valuable export markets. Contemporary attention was focussed on it, both as an ancient manufacture and because it made an expensive product. 'The most artificial (*ie* ingenious) and beneficial commodity made of wool is cloth', wrote a pamphleteer, using the word in contrast to the new draperies and other cheaper fabrics; 'the finer the cloth be, the more persons are employed about it, and the benefit of it the greater. . .there are many more people employed, and much more profit made and money imported by this manufactury alone, than by all the other manufactures of England put together'. This was in fact an exaggeration to the point of absurdity, for the market for cheaper cloth was much larger than that for the fine western product, and the serges made in Devon and west Somerset alone exceeded in volume the production of Wiltshire, east Somerset, and Gloucestershire. Yorkshire, too, was supplying large home and foreign markets with kerseys and coarse broadcloth.

After 1720 the generally high level of prosperity was not uniformly maintained. Some overseas markets declined, and competition both from Yorkshire and some foreign centres became more severe in the cheaper sectors of the trade. As in earlier periods, wars took their toll, and the outbreak of the American war led to difficulties in several Wiltshire towns. Nevertheless, the last twenty years of the hand-worked industry, 1770–1790, were years of recovery; the home market was increasing as the population rose in numbers and prosperity, and the superfine sector received an important boost by the introduction of the cassimere, a narrow twilled cloth of high quality, patented by Francis Yerbury of Bradford in 1766. Lighter and less heavily-milled than broad medley cloth, it was an instant success.

Early in the century, the only other district which competed directly with this one in the production of Spanish cloths (now more usually called medleys) was that part of Gloucestershire which lay below the Cotswolds scarp, from Wotton-under-Edge to Dursley. But the main Gloucestershire product was piece-dyed cloth, much of which was exported to the Levant. Salisbury's contribution to that trade was a fairly high-grade cloth; its export, still important in the late 17th century, had dwindled almost to nothing by 1711 in the face of French competition and, though cloths called Salisburys continued to go to the Levant, they were made in Gloucestershire. The city itself turned to the manufacture of flannels, which flourished there for most of the century.

The production of medleys occupied much of the remainder of the clothing district. An act of 1727 provided that medleys should be measured at the fulling mill by an inspector, who was to charge 2d a cloth. In both counties the justices laid down divisions for this purpose. The Wiltshire mills included the stretch from South Newton on the Wylye, up to Chippenham and Slaughterford in the north, and Seend in the east. In Somerset the divisions included, not only the Frome valley and the mills in and near Shepton Mallet and Bath, but also mills in the Chew Valley at Harptree, Chew Magna, Litton and Littleton. Cloths continued to be milled in this far western division until 1770. Some parts of Wiltshire – the immediate area of Salisbury, some mills near Calne, and Malmesbury and Castle Combe were making cloths other than medleys – flannels at Salisbury, serges and druggets at Devizes and Calne, and Gloucestershire-type cloths at Malmesbury and Castle Combe. The latter died out about mid–century, but the area otherwise remained remarkably the same in extent as it had been in the 16th century.

Defoe, in his *Tour through England and Wales,* gave an enthusiastic account of the trade in medleys, though he included in his account places certainly not noted for it, such as Castle Cary, Wincanton, and Mere. Frome excited his particular admiration. Devizes, full of wealthy clothiers, had 'lately run pretty much into the drugget-making trade'. Trowbridge and Bradford were 'the two most eminent towns in that part of the vale for the making fine Spanish cloths, and of the nicest mixtures. From these towns south to Westbury and to Warminster. . .the finest medley Spanish cloths, not in England only but in the whole world are made. . .'. He was told at Bradford that clothiers were sometimes worth from £10,000 to £40,000.

Most clothiers lived in the towns, where their houses still form an impressive witness to Defoe's account. Hardly any have external features much earlier than 1700 in date, for no prestige was then gained from living in an old house. If a substantial house of a Tudor or Stuart predecessor was worth retaining, it could be brought up-to-date by re-fronting, as the Houltons did to the old Langford house at Trowbridge c1700. Soon after, however, they built two houses on land adjoining, in the latest style, and this was much more typical. All the towns contain notable examples, seen at their best where a group remains intact, as at Woolley Street in Bradford, the Parade in Trowbridge, St Mary Street in Chippenham, the Green in Calne, and Long Street in Devizes. Sometimes their elaboration makes one speculate whether older-fashioned or poorer contemporaries did not regard them as brash. The Courts at Holt, built by a clothier, John Phelps, soon after 1703 and, according to Pevsner, wildly overdone in all its details, reminds us that clothiers still lived in some villages, and good houses are to be seen at Beckington, Rode, Hilperton, and elsewhere. Occasionally a clothier would live adjoining a fulling mill: Nicholas Pearce of Widdenham near Colerne had cloth stolen from his racks in 1731, and the Everett and Adlam families, at Horningsham and Bull Mill, Crockerton respectively, are other examples.

Some clothing families rose from the ranks of prosperous weavers, and especially from master clothworkers, who themselves were frequently employers of a number of journeymen shearmen. It would be an obvious progression for such men to invest profits in the purchase of wool, to start an independent trade, probably beginning with cheaper cloth, while still taking work on commission. William Temple the elder, who died at Trowbridge leaving a handsome fortune in 1736, began in this way; his obituary in the *Gloucester Journal,* probably written by his son, conjectured that he would have excelled in the field of literature 'had his education been as refin'd as his faculties were strong'. It was equally possible to invest money made at another trade in producing cloth. The account book of Joseph Udall, a Melksham grocer, shows that he sent 16 cloths to Blackwell Hall in the autumn of 1759. Thomas Beaven was a clothier and maltster at Melksham in 1738, and John Whiting was innkeeper, shopkeeper, and clothier at Shepton Mallet in 1740. Other combinations are known. Some clothiers came from established local families, often ones that had made money earlier in the trade. The Houltons of Trowbridge had younger sons who were clothiers, long after the senior line had achieved gentry status, and Thomas Long was a clothier at Melksham although he stood second in succession to, and eventually inherited, the widespread estates of the Longs of South Wraxall. Others came from prosperous families elsewhere; the Baskervilles at Bradford and the Mortimers at Trowbridge were related to landed families in east Wiltshire. Entry into the trade could be by apprenticeship. Wiltshire indentures made between 1720 and 1760 show that 75 boys were apprenticed to clothiers. The custom of apprenticeship was stronger in the corporate towns, and more than half took place in Salisbury and its neighbourhood and in Devizes. Some apprentices were from genteel families, others the sons of yeomen or tradesmen: all their parents had the ability to pay a premium, most of which ranged from £20 to £50. But six were of £100 or more, the highest the 200 guineas paid to Isaac Greene of Trowbridge in 1758.

Nevertheless it was possible to enter the trade without formal training. When Samuel Brewer of Trowbridge gave up trade in 1723, his house was advertised to let as fit for a clothier, and the tenant could obtain instruction from a neighbour if necessary. Partnership too could provide circumstances in which a young man might learn the trade while employing his capital, and many businesses were carried on between two or three partners. In 1771 an anonymous gentleman offered to put £1,000 or £1,500 into any extensive trade as a partner, and in 1784 a Salisbury clothier advertised for a partner with £2,000–£5,000 to put into his business, knowledge of the trade being unnecessary. Francis Yerbury's opinion of 1753 was probably true: 'Let a Spaniard be sent over to Bradford tho' ever so great a Dunce, if he have but money and wool he may in a few months probably make as good cloth as the eldest Tradesman in the town. . . People never bred to the trade, and more, Boys have entered into it and have cut as good or better figure than many who have been regular bred to it, all which greatly depends upon the hands they employ'.

Westbury House, Bradford.

Yerbury himself came of a family which had then been in the trade for two centuries, and was to continue in it for another 70 years. Other families, such as the Goldneys of Chippenham, the Clarks of Trowbridge, the Wanseys of Warminster and the Sheppards of Frome had connections with the trade of two centuries or more. People such as these were able to put money made in good times into property or investments such as turnpikes, canals, banks or public funds. New entrants, whether they had raised the necessary capital by frugality while workpeople, or from family sources, were more vulnerable to the ups and downs of trade, and bankruptcies were common. Samuel Plummer, who came to Trowbridge from Beckington in 1752, took leases of workshops and of the fulling mill at Ladydown, but was bankrupt within the year; Henry Cam, bankrupt at Bradford in 1749, was the son of a weaver, and brother of Samuel Cam, who died in 1792 worth £80,000.

41

With these, we may contrast the bankruptcies of men such as Peter Temple of Bishopstrow in 1745 or Joseph Houlton of Trowbridge in 1758, both from prosperous families with long histories in the trade. George Wansey commented wryly on Temple as one of many who had come to grief with greater beginnings than his own: 'a person who occupied this very closet I now enjoy. . .my father's apprentice: He began the world with a plentiful Fortune I suppose not so little as £2500. . .reduced to nothing, several thousands of pounds of other persons gone with it. . .He became a Bankrupt, fled for his life into foreign parts'. Others could come and make a success: John Waldron, a Devonian, appointed minister of the Conigre church at Trowbridge in 1744, built up a business which lasted into the factory period, while a marriage connection brought the brothers Benjamin and Matthew Jervis from their genteel Staffordshire background to Trowbridge rather earlier in the century. Another immigrant who prospered was Humphrey Relph, who came from Sedgefield, county Durham, to Bradford.

The humble backgrounds of some clothiers led to regular sneers: a pamphleteer of 1727 wrote, 'I have heard it with good reason declared, that *Sir Edward Hungerford's* Kitchen, train'd up and fed, many a poor Boy of *Bradford,* who after passing the *Snap-reel* and Warp'd at the *Long-bar,* in due time became a topping *Clothier.* Do not we see a Baker's and Maltster's Sons, by the help of that *Instrument,* daily set up for Gentlemen'. James Bodman, a prosperous weaver turned unsuccessful clothier, encapsulated the point of view, which must have been common in the mouths of the workpeople, in his *History of Trowbridge,* published in 1814: 'there are few rich families in the town but what came from poor extraction, and few poor ones but spring from rich ancestors. . .there are many well built-family houses. . .the major part of them are occupied by new families, who have from small properties accumulated ample fortunes, while the builders of them are lost in name or reduced in circumstance'. It was very far from universally true.

After 1700, account and pattern books survive for a few clothiers, and new sources such as newspapers and fire insurance policies add to our knowledge. Some accounts include balance sheets, showing the total amount of stock-in-trade, *ie* the value of raw materials, cloth being made, cloths not sold, implements, and debts still owing, minus, of course, debts owed. George Wansey of Warminster, who made mainly middle-grade and cheap cloth, reckoned his stock at £4,037 in 1753; by 1761 it had increased to £6,010. These figures do not give us his total fortune, for that included property, household goods and, possibly, other investments. William Hussey of Salisbury had £21,391 in trade in 1753; he also owned property worth £5,310 and had £7,028 owed to him, although he owed (not in trade) £8,267. This left him a fortune of £25,463 not including household goods, horses, and plate. By the time he ceased clothing in 1764 he had only £10,132 in trade, but had £31,398 in investments, mainly government stock, and £18,877 in property. Hussey insured the stock in his Salisbury premises for £5,300 in 1751, a far larger sum than most clothiers in the middle part of the century. They were more likely to insure for a few hundred pounds only; George Wansey only insured for £200 stock in 1759, a reminder that so much of what a clothier owned was out with weavers, millmen, or clothworkers, or in London waiting to be sold. There was no doubt also a tendency to under-insure. Some did, however, insure cloth in the hands of factors in London.

A good picture of a moderate business comes from some balance sheets of the Chippenham partnership of Margaret Goldney and her two sons, Gabriel and Thomas, entered into in 1763, when their stock was reckoned at £3,000. A balance sheet of 1764 includes three bags and 456 lb of Spanish wool, £147: wool for 25 pieces picking, scribbling, and spinning, £250: 31 chains at the weavers, £465: 24 cloths being burled and milled, £465: nine cloths being dressed, £172: 32 cloths in factor's hands, £661: and £1,331 owing from the factor. These, with small sums for stocks of soap, dyestuffs, oil, cards, and a horse, brought the gross value in trade up to £3,640. Against this were set £500 which the partners had borrowed on bond; debts to suppliers of commodities, and for work done on commission, £745: and £469 for bills drawn on their London factor and others.

This left £1,885 in stock. The next year they were able to increase their net stock to £2,157 and divide £225 among themselves for profit. Another balance sheet for the same firm (though with only two partners) shows that stock-in-trade had increased to £10,210 by 1796.

The pattern book of Thomas Long survives for the whole of his time in trade (1699–1728), and shows that he made 1,172 cloths, an average of 39 a year; his maximum was 70 and his minimum 22. For the first ten years he kept a note of his profits, which varied from £19 to £52, and in percentage of outlay from 6·4 to 13·3. An unknown Trowbridge clothier averaged about 120 a year between 1707 and 1726. These were modest trades compared with that of Usher and Jefferies of Trowbridge, who averaged about 290 cloths a year between 1726 and 1744. Jeremiah Awdry of Melksham sent up 1,510 cloths to his factor between 1729 and 1739, an average of 137. He did not rely only on making cloth, as he had extensive property and also farmed. A picture of a really large trade comes from the account of Anthony Methuen of Bradford in the year after he died. Between 1 June 1716 and 19 July 1717, 465 cloths worth £7,524 were sent to London, where the factor already held cloth worth £11,002. The extent of this business amply bears out what Defoe was told.

Between 1769 and 1775 John Yerbury of Bradford sent between 300 and 400 cassimeres each year; and a book from Trowbridge, possibly of Salter and Dunn, shows a trade of about the same extent in the 1780s. Another anonymous Trowbridge book contains between 100 and 200 cloths between 1776 and 1783, rising to 272 in 1785, when the clothier had begun to make cassimeres as well as medleys. John Clark of Trowbridge made almost 500 cloths a year between 1779 and 1794.

Pattern books relate to the higher end of the market. The account books of Stephen Hillman of Devizes run from 1769 to 1806: his trade was in medium-grade cloths for the eastern market – Salisburys, long Worcesters, draperies, white and striped lists – of which he made generally between 500 and 600. It is curious that even this numerically-large trade appears only moderate when compared with some claims made in the press about the weekly capacity of workshops: at Seend Head in 1756 and at Bradford in 1775, 20, and at Devizes in 1778, 30. Most advertisements speak of from six to 12 cloths a week, however.

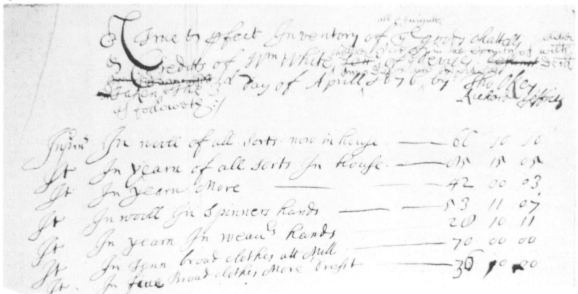

A clothier's stock-in-trade, William White of Devizes, 1676. (WRO)

ABOVE: Bowlish, Shepton Mallet. LEFT: Church Street, Warminster.
RIGHT: Pattern book of Thomas Long of Melksham: note the references to
the marks, 2 arrow and 3 arrow. (WRO)

THE

Devil drove out of the Warping-Bar;

OR, THE

Snap-Reel Snap'd.

Shewing the

MADNESS
OF THE
WEAVERS,
AND THE
Folly and Barbarity
OF THE
CLOTHIERS
In the WEST.

In a LETTER to a Gentleman of *Chippenham.*

And ſerves as a full Anſwer to a Pamphlet, lately Publiſhed; Entitled, *The Devil to do in the* WEST, &c.

LONDON:

Printed, and Sold by the Bookſellers of *London* and *Weſtminſter,* in the Year 1727.

Price 6 d.

[Handwritten inventory document:]

one Dough troce two horse and Lumber — 51 - 5 - 0

In the Brew House: It one Braſs Fornace with Iron grates one Braſs Boyler with the grate, one Maſhing Tubb three Trinders two tubbs four bouls & Lumber — 2 - 18 - 0

In the working Shops: It Seventy Seven Couple of Handles — 9 - 6 - 6

It Twenty pair of Shears att — 12 - 0 - 0

It five pair of Shears more att — 1 - 5 - 0

It four Shear Boards with the Clooeing trigsalls Straws and paſtboards to ye Same — 2 - 10 - 0

It four Dubling Boards four teesalls and four Troughs — 1 - 10 - 0

It Eight Sotts of Leades weight 400 tt — 2 - 2 - 0

It Stags for 77 Couple of Handles twelve Breasts four Cotten Beards eight kinklocks, eight Bootts Sixteen Staves of Trigsalls and all other Lumber — 2 - 10 - 0

It one Boott Boaded and the Bodding belonging to the Same — 1 - 7 - 6

It the Cloth press Ropes pully twelve planks and all other belonging to him — 10 - 1 - 0

It fourteen Duzen of parchments and three Duzen of pastboards att — 8 - 6 - 0

It the Setting Rocks Lumber &c — 5 - 10 - 0

It his Wearing Apparrell both woollen and Linen — 5 - 0 - 0

It his Table Linen — 1 - 0 - 0

ABOVE: *The Snap-Reel Snap'd,* 1727. RIGHT: Pattern book, unknown Trowbridge clothier, 1780. (WRO) BELOW: Contents of the workshop of James Bartlee of Trowbridge, clothworker, 1715. (WRO)

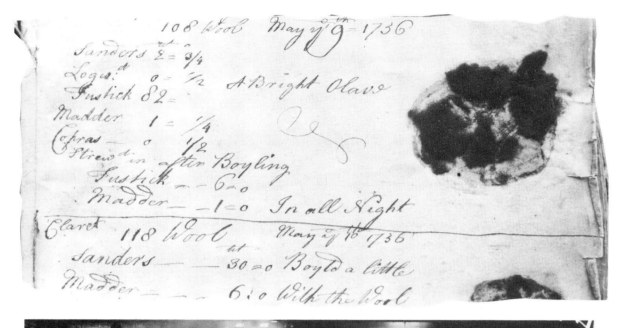

ABOVE: Dye-recipe book of John Clark of Trowbridge, 1756. BELOW: Dyehouse, Salters, Trowbridge, 1913, but an 18th-century scene apart from the steam-valve. (Both WRO)

Extreme Good Goods

Better business records give us much more detail about how a clothier ran his business. If he used English wool (and most did to some degree), it was generally bought sorted from a woolstapler, and by the middle of the 18th century markets were unimportant as a direct source for the clothiers. A number of substantial staplers were established in and around the clothing districts. Stephen Hillman of Devizes acted both parts, bringing in wool from Sussex and Hereford and selling it to clothiers in Devizes and Trowbridge. Spanish wool came mainly to London. It was a common practice for Blackwell Hall factors to act as agents, sending down the wool and setting off its cost against the cloth sold. Some firms, however, bought direct from the importers: Stevens and Bailward of Bradford dealt with a Spanish firm, though they also employed a broker in London to inform them of what was available. The wool was brought down by waggon from London and this, with taking up the cloth, supported several large carrying businesses, such as those of the Claveys of Frome and the Clarks of Trowbridge. Some Spanish wool came into Bristol and Exeter, and Usher and Jeffries of Trowbridge bought at both places in the 1720s.

It was usual for both Spanish and English wool to be sorted by the stapler. The clothier's first job was to have it picked by hand to remove vegetable matter and pitch. It was then scoured to get rid of the natural grease: this was done by warming it in stale human urine (a natural source of ammonia, known locally as sig) mixed with water in a scouring furnace, and then by suspending the wool in a basket in running water. This process had to be carried out at a dyehouse adjoining a stream, so that even clothiers who had their own dyehouses had to put this part of their work out to specialist dyers, if they did not have running water. If the wool was to be dyed, dyeing with natural dyestuffs and the necessary mordants to make them take was a complex process, and many clothiers sent their work to specialist dyers, though the larger clothier's houses often had a dyehouse on the premises. Dyestuffs were largely exotic in origin, and were bought from specialist firms of drysalters, often based in London or Bristol. Some, however, set up locally: Edward Davis of Bradford had a warehouse there and a mill at Avoncliff, which he used for grinding the dyestuffs, the river being used for transport between the two sites. Billingsley and Bowles had a logwood mill at Stoke Lane near Shepton Mallet until they gave up in 1784, and in that year also, a mill capable of manufacturing 200 tons of woad a year was for sale at Chewton Keynsham. Woad, which was used both as a dye and to provide a ground for other dyes, especially indigo, was grown extensively around Keynsham.

Dye liquors were made from recipes known for various colours, and a good dyer was one who could match patterns exactly. In the late 18th century, Ann Down had a great reputation for this at her Corsley dyehouse, especially important because it was a piece dyehouse, where cloths were dyed. This was a specialised business differing from wool dyeing. Dyehouses were equipped with copper furnaces for heating the liquor and materials, and wooden vats for them to stand in, and often also had a mill to grind indigo. The large public dyehouse at Eden Vale, Westbury, had four furnaces and five vats in 1785. In 1810 a firm at Coleford near Frome advertised wrought iron furnaces at one third the price of copper.

After wool had been scoured, and dyed unless it was to be made white, it had to be dried. In good weather this was accomplished by exposing it outside; a Salisbury clothier in 1687 spread the wet wool on the bags in which Spanish wool came. In wet weather wool could be dried in a fire stove, a stone building like a small tower, in which the wool was laid on slatted staging, heated by a central iron stove, with flue pipe to the apex of the roof. These were necessary at all dyehouses while some also had air or wind stoves – perforated buildings in which the wool was dried by the passage of air. It then had to be treated to open out the fibres and get out any solid dirt not removed by scouring. This was frequently done by beating it on hurdles with willow rods, but could be done mechanically. Jeremiah Cray of Horningsham had invented a machine driven by water in the late 17th century, and one account of making cloth in 1749 speaks of a machine like a bolting mill called a willy. Such machines, often also called whaums, were evidently common in clothier's workshops in the second half of the century, but hand beating persisted as well.

To make it work without breaking, the wool was now oiled. Many sorts of oil are known to have been used, even stale butter but, for the higher grades of cloth, it was necessary to have olive oil imported from the Mediterranean, known as Gallipoli oil. This was mainly bought in London or Bristol, and was used in considerable quantities, as a gallon would be used for every 20 or 30 lb of wool. Wool was spread in layers, and the oil sprinkled from a watering pot over each in turn.

The next stage was to have the wool scribbled, which was done in the master's workshop by his own scribblers. It was said in 1794 that scribbling offered employment to 'men advanced in age or by accident or by misfortune disabled from working in other occupations which require bodily exertion'. George Wansey employed only one when he started in 1737, and by 1752 had increased to ten; workshops at Bowlish near Shepton Mallet were said to have space for twenty scribblers in 1786. All sales of clothier's goods include scribbling horses: frames covered with leather leaves set with iron teeth, over which the wool was drawn with hand cards. After scribbling, the wool was ready to be spun.

Market spinners persisted until the introduction of machinery, frequently in places outside the main clothing area, such as Minety, Malmesbury, Dauntsey, and Swindon. Their yarn probably went to the smaller producers, but the majority of spinning was done by women directly employed by clothiers. This too occupied a wide area, for it took a number of spinners to make the yarn for one cloth. It was regular for clothiers to have a spinning house in a distant village, which could evidently be a portable shed, since one was included in the bankrupt effects of Brooks and Randall of Melksham in 1783. Thomas Long of Melksham had a house at Yatesbury, and John Serle of Shepton Mallet had one there in 1788, some 40 miles from home. In 1783 an employee of Mr Jesser of Salisbury was robbed of the money he was taking to pay spinners at Everleigh. Dealing with spinners evidently required special skill, for a man who had been used to doing it advertised his services in 1784, and the next year Henry Wansey advertised for 'a spinning house man who understands taking in of yarn'. In 1787 and 1790 Salisbury clothiers prosecuted spinners at Bulford, Winterslow, and Pitton for failing to work up the materials delivered to them.

The spinner's first task was to card the wool with hand cards, which were normally supplied by the clothier. The Dutch immigrants had brought improved methods of making cards, and imports had ceased. In the 18th century Frome was the greatest centre of cardmaking in England, and was said to supply the Yorkshire clothing towns. James Matthews, a Frome cardmaker whose business was begun by his father over 80 years earlier, died in 1784 worth £80,000. One Frome maker is said to have employed over 400 hands. Towards the end of the century cardmaking was mechanised; the machinery first appeared in the west at Dursley (another important cardmaking town) in 1792, and by 1794 Rawlings and Gregory had it at Frome. Clothiers habitually sold worn hand cards, which could then be re-used in making lower grade cloth.

Spinning was done on the great wheel, and the yarn was then wound off on to the reel which made it into skeins. Reels with a simple device to measure the length of a skein were in use by 1727, when one figured in the title of a pamphlet, *The Snap-Reel Snap'd*. The yarn for the warp was spun harder than that for the weft, to give it extra strength. Warping was carried out by the weaver to whom the work was given out; this was done on the clothier's premises, and involved winding the skeins on to bobbins and then measuring out the warp, using a device called a warping bar and skirme, the exact nature of which is not known. Some warps were made of doubled yarn, and it was presumably for this that the twisting mills mentioned after 1700 were used. Before putting it into the loom, the weaver also had to size the warp yarn, that is dip it into a thin glue, and allow it to dry, by hanging it out on poles. Then he had to set it up in a loom which was sometimes his own property, but could also be rented from his master or a third party. Even parts of looms could be rented: a Seend slaymaker had slays worth £20 let out to various weavers in 1713. The loom stood in a room which he called his shop which, if he was prosperous, might contain another loom or two, let out by him or used on his behalf. If he had children they could be employed to wind the weft skeins on to quills, the local name for the bobbins to go into the shuttle. Before doing this, the skein had to be wetted, as good weaving was said to require damp weft.

Wool drying stove, Horningsham.

After the clothier had checked the cloth, known at this stage as the say or flannel, it had to be scoured to get rid of the oil and size. This process was carried out at the fulling mill, using the stocks for a fairly short period, on a cloth which had been wetted with a stale mixture of sig and pig's dung. As it had to be handled several times in this state, the operation must have been far from pleasant. When it was clean it was burled, a job done by women, generally at the mill and while the cloth was still wet. They used burling irons, like tweezers, to remove knots and loose

49

threads. Burling was done on commission; the master burlers were generally men, who employed the women and rented space at the mills. After burling, some cloths were scoured again, this time using fuller's earth. The cloth was then fulled, a job usually carried out by specialised millmen, who rented their mills and worked on commission. Clothiers appear to have regularly sent their cloths to the same mill over long periods. George Wansey's went to Crockerton early in the century, and Stephen Hillman's to Calstone later. Prices ranged from 2s 6d to 4s a cloth. The clothier supplied the heavy oil soap which by now was the common medium for fulling fine cloths, though for coarse ones fuller's earth or sig could be used. Some clothiers ran fulling mills themselves, like Francis Yerbury of Bradford, who advertised for journeymen millmen for his mill at Avoncliff in the 1770s. Moving cloth to and from the mills must have been expensive, and Yerbury was able to send his cloth down to his mill by boat. Although the fulling mill was almost universally water-driven, it was possible to have a horse-driven mill; one was for sale at Salisbury in 1784.

From fulling was a tricky operation: although it relied on the heat produced by the rapid action of the stocks, the cloth had to be taken out regularly and 'readed', that is pulled out square to see if it was shrinking regularly – if not, more soap could be added to parts which needed it. Richard Brooks, a Devizes clothier who ran a mill at West Lavington, described the method, and the errors which could arise in fulling, in *Observations on the Art of Milling Broad and Narrow Cloth,* published in 1743. He claimed to have invented a method of eliminating them by a device called a regulator, but he died soon after, and no more is known of it. Cloths took many hours to achieve the right degree of felting and shrinkage, which was often about a third of the length and almost half the width, so that mills had to work day and night.

From fulling, the cloth was taken to the tenter rack, usually adjoining the mill, to be stretched and dried. The stretching, to eliminate errors in weaving and fulling which left the cloth other than square, was frequently overdone (pulleys could be used at the ends of the pieces), and led to endless disputes between the clothiers and the factors and drapers. So too did the question of measurement, the factors alleging that they lost money because the cloths were shorter when dried, though they had to pay for a length measured while the cloth was still wet. A bitter dispute was ended by a compromise, which allowed any buyer to have the cloth wetted and measured again, embodied in an act of 1714. 'We have the privilege' wrote a firm of factors with deep sarcasm in 1796, 'of again putting it in water to try if it has been improperly stretch'd, and to bring it back to a proper substance'.

It was at the mill that the cloths were measured and sealed by the inspectors appointed under the Act of 1727. This apparently still had real significance in 1746, when the Wiltshire justices ordered the inspectors to guard against fraud, arising from the practice of weaving a forrel into a cloth half way along and then cutting it into two and selling it as half cloths; they were to measure and seal each half. Actual measuring and sealing was last known to have been done at Clifford's Mill, Beckington, and Lullington Mill in 1770. Inspectors continued to be appointed in both counties at least until the early 19th century, but their only duty was to collect 2d for each cloth, the millmen supplying the figures.

Racks were frequently to be found away from mills, for some processes could be done when cloth was damp, by burlers who worked at their own houses, or by clothworkers. A map of Salisbury in 1716 shows a rack close near St Edmund's Church, while Milford Hill was another place where there were many racks, as we know from advertisements offering rewards for the recovery of stolen cloth. Cloth was vulnerable to theft from racks, and the rewards offered were high – 100 guineas by two Salisbury firms after eight cloths were cut from theirs in 1791. In the late part of the century, when fancy patterns were popular on cassimere, the towns must have presented a gaudy appearance; of two cloths stolen out of John Yerbury's racks at Bradford in 1778, one had a narrow pink stripe between two white ones on a sage green ground on which were black and buff spots, the other had a broad pearl-coloured stripe with green and white spots on it and a lead coloured stripe with orange and white spots. It is a pity that no artist ever recorded such a scene.

The finishing of fine cloth was done by raising the nap on the face of the cloth, done by drawing wooden frames, called handles, set with teazle-heads over its surface while it was damp, and then

Tellisford Mill, redrawn from a photograph of 1879.

shearing the nap off. It was a skilled and complex process, and the only detailed information about it, contained in the book of George Wansey I, c1700, is not clear. The first stage was to raise the nap while the cloth was stretched over a board, with four courses of handles – possibly the handles had to be changed as they took up damp from the cloth, or it may be that handles in different stages of wear were used in succession. This process was repeated once or twice, and was known, later in the century at least, as dubbing – boards for it appear in most sales of clothier's goods. It was followed by more raising called single work, probably done in only one direction, which involved the use of up to 12 courses. After a first cut with the shears, called a kerf, it was subjected to mosing, which was probably the process also known as rowing or perching, not done over a board, but when the cloth was hanging from a bar or perch. This was done twice or three times with a cut after each, and the cloth was put in the rack after each cut. Two further cuts ended the work on the surface of the cloth, and then the wrong side was cut once. The whole sequence involved betwen 30 and 50 hours of work, depending on the quality of the cloth.

In the last days of hand raising in the early 19th century, a device called a timmy nog, with rollers on which the stretched cloth could be fed forward, was brought into use.

The teazles used by clothworkers were not the common field teazles, but the hard variety with hooked spikes called *Dipsacus fullonum*. These had presumably been grown as a crop for this purpose since mediaeval times. In the 18th century this was mainly done in Somerset, where it still survived until recent years. The heads, graded by size into kings and middles, were sold to the clothiers and clothworkers in packs, and were expensive: Stephen Hillman spent over £200 on them in four years. In 1772 the clothiers and clothworkers of the three western counties met at Trowbridge to consider their high price, which they blamed on speculators who monopolised the market, and set up a committee to import cheaper ones from France and Holland. It is not known how long this lasted, but home production did not cease. In the boom after the Napoleonic wars, teazles sold for £20 a pack, but in 1829, when it had dropped to £2 10s, the growers were said to be ready to abandon them. The account books of William Sage, a Trowbridge teazle merchant, show that prices varied a good deal in the 1850s and '60s, no doubt depending on the crop. Sage bought teazles from various places in Somerset and Gloucestershire, but he also bought them, and grew crops himself, at places near Trowbridge.

The large quantities of teazles required for raising needed ventilated storage so that they would dry after being used on damp cloth. A handle house, apparently a shed with slatted sides, was a necessary adjunct to a clothier's or clothworker's workshops, and houses and the staging in them were frequently sold among their effects.

Raising the nap mechanically, by using teazles set in the drum of a gig mill, was introduced in the late Middle Ages. Although forbidden by statute in the 16th century, its use had persisted in Gloucestershire and in the northern-most part of Wiltshire. In the 18th century there were gigs at Ford Mill and Duncombe Mill, both in North Wraxall, and at Widdenham Mill near Colerne. Another gig mill was at Bulkington, which was used by the Devizes clothier Stephen Hillman to produce goods for the East India trade. It is curious that it caused no trouble at a place which, though remote, was near the centre of the clothing district, for an attempt to introduce a gig at Horningsham in 1767 led to its destruction by a mob of 500 shearmen. William Everett and his family had been engaged at Heytesbury in making goods similar to those from Gloucestershire, including the heavy coatings called Bath beavers, and had sent them to be gigged at a distance. A correspondent in the Salisbury paper, defending Everett's action after the riot, pointed out that, by installing the gig, he was doing at home work that was hitherto done elsewhere, but nothing more is known of its use until near the end of the century.

The iron shears used to shear the nap weigh some 30 lb, and appear too clumsy to do such a delicate job, especially as the pairs that survive are not ground to a fine edge as they would have been when in use. The raised cloth was stretched over a padded board curved to fit the lower blade; the shears were placed horizontally on it, with the lower blade weighted with lead weights, so that it sank slightly into the cloth. The other was then moved by wooden handles so that it caught the nap against the stationary one and, by moving the shears gradually across the cloth from list to list and then moving the cloth across the board lengthwise, the whole surface was dealt with. Pictures of the process usually show two men working across the board; possibly they took half of the width each, but it is more likely that one is following the other in the two successive kerfs mentioned in some of Wansey's descriptions.

It seems that the men in a clothworking shop worked in teams; in 1772 an advertisement sought a shearman to be foreman in a shop of two, three, or four companies. Shearboards are mentioned in pairs in sales, and the number of shears was in proportion – two pairs to 30 at Frome in 1781, three to 42 at Melksham in 1789, and six to 57 at Beckington in 1783. Shears were classified according to their use; Edmund Grant of Bradford Leigh had first kerfs, middle wools, and later kerfs in his shop in 1704. The shears were presumably made locally, possibly at the old-established iron works at Nunney. Grinding them was a specialised occupation carried out generally at water-driven edge-tool mills. A Trowbridge shear grinder rented the mill at Farleigh

Hungerford in the middle of the century, and other edge-tool mills were at Bratton and Seagry. In 1793 five shear-grinders advertised that they were increasing their charges for new shears, grinding, and steeling, and abolishing all fees to shearmen except 1d a pair for grinding.

After dressing, cloths were mended (filling in holes caused by missing threads, called drawing), brushed, and then pressed to give a gloss to the surface. This was done in a screw-press into which the cloth was folded between paper or parchment sheets. Pressing could be done hot, by inserting iron plates heated in an oven at several places in the cloth. The presses were valuable pieces of equipment, designed to exert great pressure; some advertised in 1790 had screws of three and four inches in diameter and four feet long. Making the screws was a specialised occupation – the stock of James Watts of Frome, press-screw maker, was advertised in 1781. After pressing, the clothier's mark and name were put on the cloth and it was ready for sale.

Handle house, Studley Mill, Trowbridge.

Much cloth went straight up by road to Blackwell Hall where, in 1770, some 30 firms of factors were available to sell cloth. The names of several reveal their family connections in our area – Davis and Dowding at Trowbridge, Hall, Cockell and Wilkins at Westbury, Everett at Heytesbury, Sheppard and Jesser at Frome. With these, local clothiers would make arrangements regarding commission and credit. A clear picture of a factor's relationships with his clothiers comes from the letter book (1763–7) of James Elderton, who came from the Frome area. Elderton was anxious to form connections with clothiers: in 1764 he wrote to Samuel Ledyard of Trowbridge, 'use all the arguments with Mr. Cook [Samuel Cook, another Trowbridge clothier] you are master of to engage him in our favour, as the late worthy Mr. Partridge [a rival factor] departed this life this morning, and should be glad if you would speak to Messrs. W. and T. Pitman at Bradford. . .if you could in any way take a ride to Bruton, to Mr. Gousborough and solicit him in our favour. . .' Elderton would offer credit and advances of money to induce a clothier to agree with him; in 1764 he asked Benjamin Peach of Westbury to enquire for a superfine clothier in Salisbury with £1,000 or £1,500 in trade to whom he could advance another £1,000. He expected his clothiers to deal only with him as far as London sales went, and found it especially galling that they should go to another factor while they owed him money. 'You are sending cloths to some other person and my money is to pay for it. . .I know you make more cloth than you send to me, but I will find it out', he wrote to George Walker of Rode in 1763. George's brother, John, also excited Elderton's wrath by doubting his honesty in accounting for the cloths sold; 'do not give me any of your damn'd cant of your hypocritical religion' wrote Elderton, 'you may go to every draper and see we give you a just account, and I will pay your coach to town for so doing'.

Elderton was not particularly straightforward himself – he advised the Trowbridge partnership of Read and Wilkins to mark their cloths Read and Co, so that buyers would think they had succeeded to the trade of another eminent clothier called Read – and the bite and sarcasm of his letters must have caused deep offence. Where Hanson and Mills, another firm of factors, used such phrases as 'the cloths are not executed with your usual precision', Elderton showed no restraint – 'the worst cloth I ever saw. . .burly, thready, and as thin as a common cloth, and the spinning as big as my finger': 'a bad colour and as dirty as if dressed in a ditch': 'the coarsest worst cloth that I ever saw, I am certain it is not made of wool but dog's hair'. If a clothier remonstrated, he got more – 'you would use a factor like your shearmen or scribblers. I never was or ever will be subservient to any clothier'.

Yet Elderton would on occasions offer what appears to be good advice on making the cloths, and had much to suffer from his clothiers. A particular cause of complaint was that they failed to match the patterns he sent. In 1764 he ordered 24 liveries from Nicholas Cockell of Chapmanslade – 'desire you will be very particular to make them very neat stout good cloths, put fine wool in them, and don't strain them more than just strait in the rack, as they will every piece be shrunk. . .they must be dyed to the 20th part of a shade as to patterns'. When this and a later order failed to match the patterns, the buyer wanted to cancel 'but I told him the whole order was dyed. I find they cannot give the price, they want to have them made in Yorkshire but he told me what was already dyed he would take and have the others made in Yorkshire. I know there is but few of them dyed, but I would have you write me in your next of about 35 or 40 of them dyed'.

Elderton had clothiers making cloth in all grades, and was always able to threaten those at the lower end of the trade with Yorkshire competition, especially as he considered their work was poor; 'we have been cruelly used, damn'd vile, by our coarse makers and their dyers, we had at one time the very best coarse orders, but instead of executing their orders they were all spoilt'. Several of these makers came from the Chapmanslade area, and Elderton blamed bad dyeing: 'we have reason to curse a certain dyehouse' he wrote in 1769, meaning apparently the Cockell family's dyehouse at Bissford near Corsley. In 1768 he complained to the clothier Nicholas Cockell, 'Your cloth gets a very indifferent repute. . .what sort of oil do you use, your cloth feels like Yorkshire cloth milled up in the grease. . .the agent who wanted 50 at 6s. 9d. said he would not put such coarse, big spun, ill dress'd, greasy Yorkshire stuff in his shop if you would let him have it for 4s.'

It is clear from Elderton's letters that there was a finely graded scale of cloths by price, clearly understood by buyers and sellers, as well as by name. To John Huntley of Westbury he wrote, 'I wish I could persuade you to keep on the 14s. and 12s. sorts and a few at 11s.', and to the same clothier, 'The very best cloths that are made in England will fetch no more than 16s. a yard made with wool at 2s. 7d. or 2s. 8d. per pound, the very best that are made at Bradford and Trowbridge will sell for no more than 16s., and a great deal sold for 15s. 6d. to the best houses. . .this No. 1156 is a pretty good cloth and I dare say I shall get a pretty good price for him, but am afraid never 16s. . . .if it sells for 15s. 6d. it will be its full value'. The names for the various grades also appear – superfines, best-supers, supers at the top of the scale, seconds and liveries in the middle, and toilinettes, plunkets, duffles, and beavers near the bottom. Judging by advertisements of the sales of clothier's stocks, some appear to have made cloths in all grades, and in the first directory of the district, published in 1783, a number of clothiers at Frome, Warminster, and Westbury described themselves as superfine, second and livery clothiers. On the other hand 26 in those towns and in

Bradford, Beckington, and Trowbridge claimed to be superfine clothiers. In 1770 eight firms from Trowbridge, Bradford and Melksham advertised that they did not make superfines at under 16s a yard, and that cloths marked superfine and sold for less must be inferior to theirs in quality. At Trowbridge and Melksham only, a few clothiers said they made ladies' and fancy cloths. Salisbury clothiers still made flannels, linseys, and cottons, and their range was well known by the name of Salisbury goods.

If cloths failed to sell in London, they were usually returned to the clothier. Sometimes, however, the factors held auction sales in London; Elderton's firm held them monthly in 1773, claiming that though they had to remove the names and marks, yet they were 'extreme good goods'. In 1777 John Watts of Trowbridge brought a successful action against his factor, claiming he had no right to sell cloths in this way, and gained £500 in damages.

Clothiers had other ways of disposing of their cloth besides the use of a factor. Some of the most eminent were able to set up warehouses of their own in London; Cam, Read and Co of Bradford had one in the middle of the century, and Joseph Mortimer of Trowbridge and Joseph Saunders of Bradford shared one in 1770. Others sold direct to the buyers in London. Usher and Jeffries of Trowbridge dealt directly with one London draper in 1726–7, though this upset their factors, and a London draper advertised for direct suppliers in 1781. William Temple of Trowbridge made a direct approach to a draper in 1745. After saying that the purpose of his letter was not to sound his own applause, he wrote, 'I am pretty well acquainted with the Fine Fabricks in the West, and as well satisfied none comes up to the Elegance, Beauty and Perfection of my own, on an Average'. But the purpose of his letter was to say that he had quitted Blackwell Hall 'As I am exempt from the charges incident to Blackwellhall, and a Factor, it is morally impossible a Clothier who uses their Intervention should serve you so well and so cheap as I can'. He also, incidentally, announced that he had begun to manufacture various types of cloth for the Levant trade, which he described as imitations of the French, an indication of the inroads they had made into this sector, and it is interesting to note that the better qualities of his imitations, priced at 7s–8s 6d a yard were made entirely of Spanish wool.

The direct customer of Usher and Jeffries had chosen his patterns at Bristol, almost certainly at the fair there, and it is clear that clothiers made considerable sales at fairs both to London and country customers throughout the 18th century. Elderton's firm held an auction of cloths during the first three days of Bristol fair, no doubt to take advantage of the drapers gathered there. At Salisbury a new August wholesale cloth market began in 1769, to replace the old-established twelfth market held in January.

Better postal and carrying facilities made it possible to trade without meeting. When John Hewlett of Knook advertised 'the finest dressed druggets, equal to superfine Spanish cloth in beauty' in 1727, he offered to sell wholesale or retail and to match patterns sent by letter. Several Trowbridge clothiers sold all the cloth they made in the country in the 1720s and 1730s, and the surviving account books of William Westley of Shepton Mallet show that he dealt with drapers all over the southern and western parts of England. A man with these connections might have travelled himself in search of orders, or employed someone else. In 1786 one traveller with good connections with mercers (though he travelled in hardware, nails, and hats), offered to represent a clothier, and another man sought a post as a rider in 1791.

Some clothiers were themselves able to export. George Wansey sent cloth to the West Indies, and met a Pennsylvania merchant in Bristol in 1741, a connection he thought valuable when London trade was discouraging and he had cloths on hand. It may be that such a trade was less exacting than satisfying the standards of factors, especially those with a command of language such as Elderton: Hanson and Mills told a Melksham clothier in 1795 that a cloth was 'unsaleable except for an American order owing to its being very foul'. But trading at such a distance was risky; Westley had an American venture which came to grief because of the death of his contact, and George Wansey lost £1,000 by the Lisbon earthquake of 1755.

ABOVE: Dyehouse, Courts Mill, Trowbridge, probably 18th-century. Note the ventilation by perforated brickwork and louvred top. BELOW: Wool drying stoves, Melksham; LEFT: Church Street and RIGHT: Lowbourne.

ABOVE: Workshop and dyehouse buildings behind the houses in Hill Street, Trowbridge, photographed 1922. BELOW: Bridge House, Trowbridge, with workshops behind, flanked by 19th-century factory and warehouse. (BM)

LEFT: Snap-reel for measuring yarn by the clock on the left. CENTRE: Burling iron. RIGHT: Stowford Mill. BELOW: Cloth making book of Thomas Long of Melksham, showing payments to women spinners. (WRO)

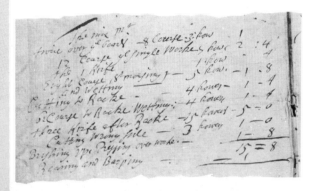

OBSERVATIONS
ON
MILLING

Broad and Narrow

CLOTH, &c.

SHEWING

I. The *many destructive Errors* that attend the common Method of Milling, and Reading or Tighting of CLOTH, during its Milling. And,

II. The *many Advantages* that accrue, instead thereof, from the Use of a *new* INSTRUMENT, called a REGULATOR.

To which is annexed,

A CERTIFICATE signed by several of the *most eminent* CLOTHIERS in the *Superfine* Trade.

By RICHARD BROOKS, *Clothier*,
Inventor of the said REGULATOR, and Patentee, at the *Devizes*, in the County of *Wilts.*

LONDON:
Printed for the Author in the Year
MDCC XLIII.

LEFT: Richard Brooks's pamphlet on fulling, 1743. (DM) RIGHT: Teazles set in a handle: this one is from a gig-mill – for hand work there would have been a handle below. CENTRE: Directions for cloth finishing c1700. BELOW: Tenter-rack still in position at Staverton, 1897. (Both WRO)

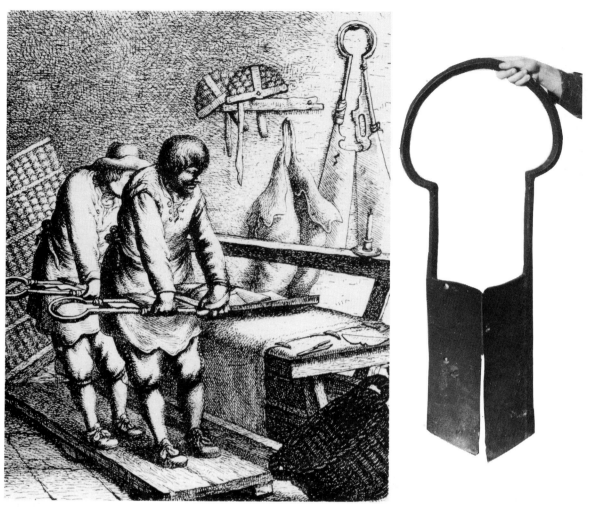

LEFT: Shearmen at work, with handles on the wall and teazles set in staging
behind, and RIGHT: the real thing. BELOW: James Elderton dresses down
a clothier, 1766. (SRO)

60

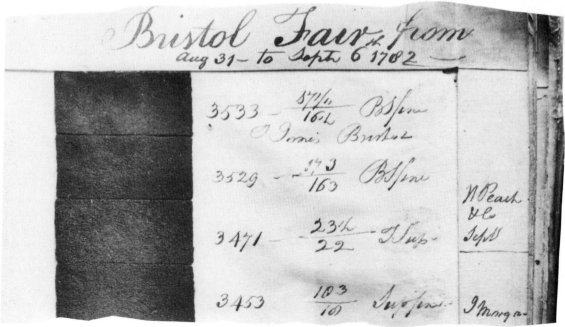

ABOVE: Account of Jeremiah Awdry of Melksham with his factor, 1739.
BELOW: Cloths sent to Bristol Fair from Trowbridge, 1782. (Both WRO)

A FUGITIVE and PILFERING WEAVER.

FLED from his Work, unfinished, and considerably in arrears, likewise pilfered and carried off several small quantities of Silk Yarn, GEORGE BEAUMONT, Weaver, a native of Melksham. If any person will communicate information by letter to Mr. Samuel Cook, of Trowbridge, where the aforesaid offender may be met with, that due justice may be administered, it would be an useful example to the trade, and Mr. Cook will thankfully defray any reasonable costs. [46

To Clothiers, Dyers,

&c.

SOMERSETSHIRE TO WIT.

WHEREAS,

EDWARD ROGERS,

Of Road,

In the said County, Weaver, was on the seventh day of April instant, deemed and adjudged to be guilty of a misdemeanor, and duly convicted before THOMAS SWYMMER CHAMPNEYS, Esq. and HENRY SAINSBURY, Clerk, two of his Majesty's Justices of the Peace in and for the said County, of having on the first day of April instant, had in his possession, in his Dwelling-house and Premises, at the said parish of Road, a quantity of wrought and unwrought Materials used in the Woollen Manufacture, consisting of three pieces of Woollen Cloth, and divers quantities of Wool and Yarn, suspected to be purloined or embezzled, and of not producing the party or parties being duly entitled to dispose of the same, of whom he bought or received the same, nor giving a satisfactory account how he came by the same Materials; for which offence, the said EDWARD ROGERS was, by the said Justices, adjudged to forfeit the sum of Twenty Pounds, pursuant to the statute in that case made and provided. Notice is therefore hereby given, that the said Cloth, Wool, Yarn, and Materials are, by order of the said Justices, deposited at the house of Mr. ISAAC RAWLINGS, in Frome-Selwood, in the said County, for the space of thirty days from the date hereof, to the end that persons having lost such Materials, or any reputable person or persons in their behalf, may come and claim the same, and in case any person or persons can prove his, her, or their property in the said Materials, upon oath or solemn affirmation to the satisfaction of two of his Majesty's Justices of the Peace for the said County of Somerset, who will meet at my Office in Frome-Selwood aforesaid, on the 14th and

ABOVE: Industrial embezzlement, 1785. BELOW: A wicked weaver of Rode, c1830: *not* an ancestor of the author but, alas, certainly a relative.

What About the Workers?

In 1756 George Wansey wrote a private reflection: 'I venerate the memory and thank God for those ancestors of mine that have gone before me, from whose labours and from whose prudence and virtue I derive many of the present conveniences and advantages I enjoy . . . above those who are forced to get their bread by the sweat of their brows and are destitute of many opportunities and advantages I have enjoyed for the improvement of my mind'. Wansey came from a pious and liberal family (he refused to acquire a profitable West Indian property because he objected to slavery), and when he wrote 'I would be a kind master to all my servants, not be pressing to have my work done at the lowest rates of anybody, but be glad to see the poor live comfortably by my work', it has a convincing ring. Yet the relationship between master and man posed problems, for it was difficult for the master to supervise the quality of spinning, weaving, and often dressing, done outside his direct control.

Elderton's complaints were frequently of thick spinning, cloth not struck up in the loom, and careless shearing. John Clark of Trowbridge, both clothier and minister, found labour relations exacerbated by his position. His workpeople were 'vulgar and low-bred people, who are often actuated by the most selfish and illiberal motives . . . many take the advantage of my being a preacher to impose upon me . . . some to whom I preach the gospel freely even spoil my work'.

Tension could arise in a number of ways. One was the clothiers' constant fear of pilferage. Spinners and weavers were able to store up small quantities of wool and yarn until they had enough to sell, usually at a price far below its value. Advertisements appeared from time to time warning against the practice; in 1741 a Trowbridge advertiser tried to get contributions towards the costs of a recent prosecution, that of 'one of those moths of the woollen manufacture, an end-gatherer', who had been whipped at Devizes, Melksham, and Trowbridge. He had bought quantities of wool and yarn, worth from 9d to 5s 6d a lb, for from 2½d to 4d. Such a man would then sell the materials to someone willing to take the risk of making them up into a cloth. A gang from Gloucestershire was active in the district in 1773. Several end collectors were punished in 1777, and 8 cwt of yarn burnt in Devizes market place, while two men from Calne were sent to prison for resisting a search of their houses. Associations to prosecute offenders were founded at Trowbridge in 1785, and at Frome by 1794, when a clothier was prosecuted and 20 guineas reward offered. In 1792 a weaver at Chittoe, who took a cloth to Melksham to be dressed, but could not give its source, went to prison for a month.

The workers complained of truck payments; paying in goods rather than money. One excuse was shortage of coin but, since the clothiers set the price of their commodities, workpeople inevitably believed that they were cheated. The same was true if the clothier, or a relative or tenant, kept a shop and expected his people to deal there. Worst of all was payment in cloth, which the workpeople had either to wear or to sell at a loss. It was illegal, but a weaver could not prosecute a master and remain employed. The clothiers said that truck was a form of credit, so that if cloth worth £2 was given, it was reimbursed by paying 1s less for each piece of work ahead.

Embezzlement and truck were chronic complaints, but the depressions to which the trade was always subject, the distress of unemployment, and the clothiers' attempt to lower wages, more often led to open trouble. This was surprisingly sporadic given the contrast in wealth and lifestyle between clothiers and workpeople. In 1677 a company of men led by a fiddler paraded through Trowbridge, in an attempt to raise wages from 6s to 6s 6d a week for a twelve-hour day. But the general prosperity of trade until after 1720 led to tranquillity, and the workpeople put up with their grievances. In autumn 1726 rioting broke out, in a period of high bread prices and cash shortage. The disturbances, at Bradford, Trowbridge and Frome, caused concern to the government, who feared that Jacobite sympathisers might exploit them. They found, however, that the weavers were mainly dissenters and wore the letters K.G.W. (King George's Weavers) in their hats. They claimed the clothiers used weights of 17 oz to the pound for spinning and lengthened the warps by three or four yards, both of which effectively lowered wages. A meeting held in London formulated remedies which were incorporated in an Act which, among other reforms, established the payment of weavers by the yard.

The more serious riots in the autumn of 1738 were apparently entirely owing to a depression in trade. Matthew Coulthurst, a Melksham clothier, gave out a warp to a weaver at a reduced rate, and a mob of weavers from the Trowbridge area arrived, and destroyed the cloth in his weavers' looms. The government was less inclined to conciliate; the ringleaders were arrested, all but one convicted, and three were hanged. By this time there was a local press in which the rights and wrongs of the affair could be discussed, and in December 1738 a writer who called himself Country Common Sense wrote an Essay on Riots for the *Gloucester Journal,* parts of which were given national prominence in the *Gentleman's Magazine.* He was Thomas Andrews, an unbeneficed clergyman of considerable property, who lived at Seend.

Andrews gave a balanced view – 'It is not fit that *Masters* should be suffer'd to oppress their *Servants,* force them to take *Goods,* in Defiance of Law, at an *Exorbitant* Price, nor enter into *Combinations* to fall their Wages, in a *Free Country.* Nor is it fit that *Servants* should be let alone to take their *own Revenge* on their Masters; 'tis *Pity,* indeed, they should be driven to it!' The last phrase struck his keynote: he recognised that the poor had grievances, and so voiced a point of view which fellow landowners could share. They saw the clothiers as exploiting the workpeople when times were good and turning them off when they were bad, so increasing the burden of the poor rates, of which, they considered, they bore too great a share. It was this attitude which had enabled the weavers to get their advice in 1726.

Three essays in defence of the clothiers all came from Trowbridge. 'Old Commonsense' admitted the weavers had grievances, but placed the blame on the Blackwell Hall factors, who kept clothiers short of money in bad times by imposing long credit. 'A Manufacturer in Wilts' defended clothiers on grounds of economic necessity: 'That the Workmen are able in a dull Season of Trade etc. when Work is scarce, etc. to make their Wages as comfortable as in a quick Time of Trade, when their hands are full, is not to be supposed: for in the Clothing Trade, as in other Employs, the Value of Labour has its Ups and Downs'. He went on to point out the small return the clothiers got on their capital, and that much cloth could be bought for less than it cost.

Longer and more extreme was a pamphlet by William Temple (under the pseudonym Philalethes), *The Case as it now stands between the Clothiers, Weavers, and other Manufacturers with Regard to the late Riot,* published in 1739. Temple complained that the Act of 1727 was deficient, because the clothiers were unable to get fair treatment before the magistrates: if they failed to pay because of bad workmanship or fraud, the weaver would win his case. This he said was particularly true in Trowbridge, where he bitterly attacked 'Tarquinius Superbus' (the clothier-justice John Cooper). 'The Manufacturers themselves are so sensible of the Partiality of a *certain Man,* that after the Determination of a certain Affair . . . in which the Master was grossly abused, the *Manufacturer* came up to his Master's Teeth in an audacious and insulting Manner and said to him, "Damn you,

you see you can do nothing with us, if we have a mind to stand Trial with you. I could have told you before the Trial came on, that I was sure to have my Money, and not to allow you any Damage". The clothier asked him, "How he could tell that?" The Manufacturer replied, "That a Friend in Court was Money in Purse" '.

Temple went on at length to point out that the industry provided employment for all capacities – the aged, children, blind and lame people – as well as able-bodied, and he claimed that families made more in wages, and had more regular work, in the clothing districts than elsewhere. His bitterest scorn was reserved for the weavers:

'The Weavers in general are the most feeble, weak and impotent of all the Manufacturers. A Male Child perhaps is found on a Dunghill, nursed up by the Parish, thro' Negligence and want of proper Care is weak and sickly, and at the Age of 8 or 10 Years is put an Apprentice to a Weaver: A Parent has a Child infirm, deform'd sickly, weak and distorted; he considers his Constitution, and how easy the Employment of a Weaver is, and puts him an Apprentice to that Trade, in which he knows his Child can acquire a comfortable Subsistance, without the Requisites in other Occupations of a healthy Body, and a strong Constitution. The Father is sensible in this Craft his Son is not exposed to hard Labour, to the Inclemencies of the Weather, to travel from Place to Place for Employment, etc. He knows if his Child is dull, Sagacity is not required; if weak, that Strength is not demanded; if sickly, Hardships are not incident; if slow and unactive, Agility is not necessary in the Occupation of a Weaver: And that by putting him to that Trade, he puts him into a capacity of obtaining a comfortable Subsistance, with scarce any human Abilities.' Such men, he said, could live cheaply, mainly in cottages built on the waste, could with an apprentice boy weave a cloth in three weeks and get about £2 for it, and could rely on wife and children from four upwards to quill for the loom and to earn several shillings a week more for spinning. Shearmen and scribblers could earn from 8s to 12s a week by working only four days, spending the other three drunk, and indeed Temple regarded it as axiomatic that few workpeople would do more than the minimum amount of work necessary to buy food and drink.

The final contribution to the debate came from Andrews, in a pamphlet called *The Miseries of the Miserable,* in which he challenged Temple's statements regarding the time taken to weave a cloth and the amounts that could be earned by spinning. At 6d a lb, he said a women could not earn more than 4d a day, if she spun all day, from six in the morning until nine at night and, since the introduction of fine spinning, children as young as the six-year-olds mentioned by Temple could not do it at all. 'He may be able' he wrote, 'to produce a *little Child* of *four* Years old *Quilling* to a Loom, tho' I would go *four Miles* to see it. He may be able to produce some *Wife* of a *favourite Workman,* who can earn 2s 6d or 3s a Week by the Spinning-Wheel, and at the same Time perform all necessary offices in the Family. He may be able to produce *Shearmen* and *Scribblers* who earn . . . from 8s to 12s per Week; but at 1d. an Hour, a Shearman must never sleep . . .'

The two points of view, vividly expressed, made an impression which recurs from time to time in later writers. Josiah Tucker, Dean of Bristol, writing twenty years after, contrasted the western industry with the Yorkshire one to the disadvantage of the West. The clothiers would inevitably be regarded as tyrants, and would be tempted by their position to be proud and overbearing. The workpeople, moved by envy, would never do more than they had to; would combine to get high wages, and would use them to increase their periods of idleness and drunkenness.

These generalisations were hardly justified. Legislation failed to remedy the grievances of the workpeople, but disturbances were few. The widespread riots of 1766 were due to the high price of bread and a suspicion that corn merchants and millers were profiting. Those of 1787 were directed against the growing practice of gathering looms into shops, so that the patterned cassimeres popular in the '80s could be woven under supervision. By that time, clothiers and workforce were beginning to see rapid changes.

THE
CASE

As it now stands, between the

CLOTHIERS, WEAVERS,

AND OTHER

MANUFACTURERS,

With Regard to the

Late RIOT, in the County of WILTS.

CONTAINING

REMARKS on a *Libel*, entitled *an Essay on Riots*, printed in the *Gloucester* Journal, *December* 19, 1738; some Observations on the Prices of Labour, in the WOOLLEN MANUFACTURE and HUSBANDRY; Considerations and Reflections on the Act for Maintaining the POOR, shewing the *Disadvantages* and *Injuries*, which arise to *Society* from it; Proofs of the Necessity of reducing the Price of Labour in our MANUFACTURES, in order to keep and extend our *Foreign Trade.*

THE WHOLE

Interspersed with Remarks on the Advantages arising from TRADE, to the Landed GENTLEMEN; the Burden which would fall on *all* by the Loss of *it.*

ALSO

Some OBSERVATIONS on the Conduct of Gentlemen and Magistrates towards *Trade* and *Manufacturers.*

IN A

LETTER to a MEMBER of PARLIAMENT.

By PHILALETHES.

LONDON:
Printed for the AUTHOR, and Sold by T. COOPER, at the *Globe,* in *Pater-Noster-Row.*
MDCCXXXIX.

William Temple's *Case,* 1739.

Man and Machine

In 1765 the only machinery a local clothier would see were fulling stocks at the mill where he sent his cloth, and a willey in his own workshop. He might have seen a gig mill at the two or three places in Wiltshire where they were used, or possibly in Gloucestershire. He might have heard that it was possible to card wool by machine, for the patent granted to Daniel Bourn of Leominster was reported in the *Salisbury Journal* in 1748. Bourn's machine, however, was first used in the cotton trade, and it was for cotton too that the first spinning machines were introduced. The spinning jenny, the one best suited for wool, was invented by James Hargreaves in 1764, and was in use with carding machines in Yorkshire in the early '70s. It first appeared in the west in 1776, when a group of Shepton Mallet clothiers installed one or more machines (the accounts differ) in the workhouse, as an experiment. They claimed the consent of their weavers, but a mob from the Frome and Warminster areas destroyed the machine. A few weeks later 50 principal clothiers at another meeting issued a statement signed by almost 100 clothiers from the two counties expressing approval of the 'spirited conduct' of the Shepton clothiers.

Support for experimental use of the jenny came from the workpeople too, but apparently only Shepton Mallet. They put a notice in the *Bath Chronicle* late in 1776 consenting to a two month trial, subject to their inspection, to see whether they were as useful as the clothiers claimed. Their findings are not known. Two makers of jennies advertised in the local press: Thomas Pyke of Bridgwater claimed to have improved on the 1776 Yorkshire models, and in the following year Thomas Prangley of Heytesbury offered any number at short notice. In 1777 too, the Salisbury paper reported that jennies were 'introducing in this city and neighbourhood with the greatest success'.

After that year, however, the makers stopped advertising, and nothing more is heard for four years. In 1777 John Cook from near Chard wrote to the Bath and West of England Society saying that the jennies had proved disappointing, and suggesting the Society should encourage improvements. This it did by offering a premium of five guineas to anyone who could 'render them equally fit for the making of fine as well as coarse cloths'. This strongly suggests that the early jennies did not answer the purpose of the fine trade, and might explain why Shepton Mallet was the scene of their introduction. They continued in use there as we know from an incident at Frome in 1781. After meetings attended by most clothiers, where the success of the Shepton scheme was mentioned, a jenny was put to work in the house of a poor man who supported himself by spinning. The clothiers argued that the workpeople themselves might get the machines and use them. One clothier dissociated himself, and sent some spinning to a village two miles away. To show their regard, his spinners came to Frome to thank him; it was Whit Monday, and a mob gathered, and destroyed the machine in the night. The report ended by saying that the Frome clothiers were sending for more machines, convinced that they would be accepted there as at Shepton Mallet.

Improvement in the jenny may have come from the north. In 1782 a Bristol correspondent of James Watt wrote: 'a capital clothier in Wilts has gotten a Man who has lived at Manchester and has made Spindles etc. for spinning Spanish Wool which answers perfectly, but cannot have his Work erected in the Country for fear of the Mob, he therefore wishes to have it set up here, but cant get a stream to answer'. He went on to suggest that Boulton and Watt should show the clothier, John Anstie of Devizes, a model steam engine, and that he could be induced to set one up at Bristol. The reference to power shows Anstie must have wanted to use carding machinery as well, for the jenny was hand-worked.

John Anstie was a clothier of considerable enterprise. He chaired meetings of the western manufacturers in 1786, to discuss the proposed Commercial Treaty with France and in 1784–88 to talk about export of wool. His trade is known to have been extensive in volume and variety, and he pioneered various types of fancy cassimere, some of which were made with a mixture of silk thread. He exported direct to France, Germany, and Portugal, and it was at least partly owing to the disturbed state of Europe that he went bankrupt, owing almost £50,000, in 1793. Ten years later he wrote a pamphlet on the necessity of using machinery in the woollen manufacture.

The large building which still stands in New Park Street, Devizes, and bears his initials and the date 1785, clearly held machinery. When his stock was sold in 1795 it contained 22 jennies; at least some had probably been there from the time it was built. In 1785 a census at Frome records four spinning jennies. Yet a Chippenham clothier considered in 1786 that to introduce machinery would be at the risk of life and fortune. In contrast, spinning machines were among the effect of Samuel Heaven, a clothier at Twerton upper mill in 1787, and in 1788 five houses said to have rooms large enough to take spinning machines were for sale at Hilperton Marsh near Trowbridge.

It was about this time that the machine called the slubbing billy was introduced in the west. It was invented in the north (western sources sometimes spell the word sloobing, which suggests a northern origin), but by whom is unknown. Its purpose was to make continuous, lightly twisted threads called slubbings, which could be transferred to the jenny to be spun into yarn. It resembled a jenny, but had an endless cloth moving round rollers, to which children carried pieces of carded wool from a carding machine (which could only produce them of a length equal to its own width), and joined them into a continuous length. These were then lightly twisted on the billy. The first certain reference comes from 1790, when George Salisbury, a spinning machine maker of Westbury Leigh, advertised that he would continue to make billies and jennies as he had usually done.

It was in that year that the introduction of spinning machinery first caused trouble. At Keynsham two manufacturers using it were threatened by a mob of colliers and their wives. The loss of wages from the abandonment of hand spinning became a regular complaint, voiced in pedestrian verse by Robert Sadler of Chippenham, whose poem *The Discarded Spinster; or a Plea for the Poor on the Impolicy of Spinning Jennies* was published in 1791. Next year it was said that women and children throughout east Wiltshire could only pick stones off the fields, and farmers and landowners considered an application to Parliament to suppress machine spinning.

But spinning and carding machinery met with little violence. In 1791 a Bratton man published an apology for a threatening letter to a Westbury clothier with a jenny at Bratton, but his complaint was that the clothier 'made a trade of teaching young hands to work the machine'. In the same year jennies featured in sales at Westbury and Trowbridge, James Ogden advertised for journeymen machine makers at Melksham, and Thomas Naish wanted a foreman who understood carding engines and billies at Trowbridge. Another carding machine maker was John Ford of Frome, who advertised that he had engaged 'a set of ingenious workmen'. At the end of 1791 he moved to Bath, where he advertised in 1792 that 20 firms of clothiers in Frome, Rode, Trowbridge, Bradford, Bath, Chippenham, Westbury and Gloucester could vouch for his workmanship. In spite of this, he went bankrupt in 1793, when his stock included billies and jennies as well as carding and scribbling engines.

A Bristol firm, Guppy and Armstrong, also made carding and scribbling engines in 1792 — interestingly, for scribbling was a job which had been done manually on the clothiers' own premises. In 1791 Joseph Phelps of Bradford converted a carding engine for scribbling; a mob demanded he should give it up, Phelps and other clothiers resisted and fired, killing three rioters, but finally gave the machine up, and it was burnt on the bridge. The Salisbury paper commented that no one had rioted against jennies in Wiltshire; they had been used at Bradford for four years, and carding machines for two, and their introduction had led to full employment. When some rioters were tried at Salisbury Assizes, Henry Wansey, Salisbury clothier and pamphleteer, printed the judge's charge to the grand jury, and added his own remarks on the utility of machinery, asserting that he and other clothiers had had to refuse orders because they could not use it. He probably meant that there was difficulty in scribbling by machine for, when another Salisbury clothier advertised in 1792 for a man to superintend carding machines and two jenny spinners, he also wanted a few good hand scribblers.

Advertisements of 1794 show how firmly-established jennies, billies and carding engines had become. John Cook of Trowbridge had 30 jennies of 60, 70, and 80 spindles, and four billies. Two machine makers at Westbury Leigh, George Salisbury and Briton Salisbury, both went bankrupt, each having several jennies of up to 100 spindles in stock. Briton Salisbury also operated a mill which contained a scribbling engine, as well as a carding engine and, when Joseph Phelps's goods were sold at Bradford after his death, they included two scribbling engines. Scribbling by machine was becoming accepted, but there is other evidence to the contrary, and resistance probably varied.

By 1795 another machine was available in the west: the shearing frame was invented by John Harmer of Sheffield in 1787, and a further patent of 1794 probably related to improvements for shearing fine cloth. A machine which replaced the most skilled was certain to encounter stern opposition. But the end of hand spinning had caused hardship all over east Wiltshire. So, in May 1794 a public meeting at the Bear in Devizes called for the suppression of machine spinning, and the parish of Marlborough took practical steps. After experimenting with the knitting of stockings and silk spinning, they decided to set up a clothier in Marlborough, who would neither spin by machine nor use machine-spun yarn. A house and workshops in the High Street and a mill at Elcot just east of the town were fitted up. A clothier from Trowbridge, Samuel Cook the younger, entered them early in 1795. He brought a carding engine up from Trowbridge, which enabled him to treble the quantity of spinning, but hand spinning cost him more and was disliked by his weavers. His advantage was that he could use scribbling and shearing machinery, which he could not do at Trowbridge. He halved his costs by the former, and saved 4d a yard by the latter. The experiment failed, Cook was bankrupt in 1799, and a similar scheme at Kintbury in Berkshire also came to nothing.

A distant factory could offer advantages; the owners of one in Lancashire thought it worthwhile to advertise it in the west in 1794. They pointed out that scribbling machines could be used. In 1795 the stock of a clothier at the one-mile stone on the Stapleton road in Bristol was for sale. It included a scribbling engine and four shearing frames, and the freedom to use any machinery. Sales at Trowbridge and Frome in that year included carding engines but not scribbling ones, and the first reference to machine scribbling at Trowbridge was in 1798.

In 1797 Frome cardmakers Allen, Hall and Co were making clothing for scribbling machines, and no more opposition is heard. Resistance now focussed on finishing machinery.

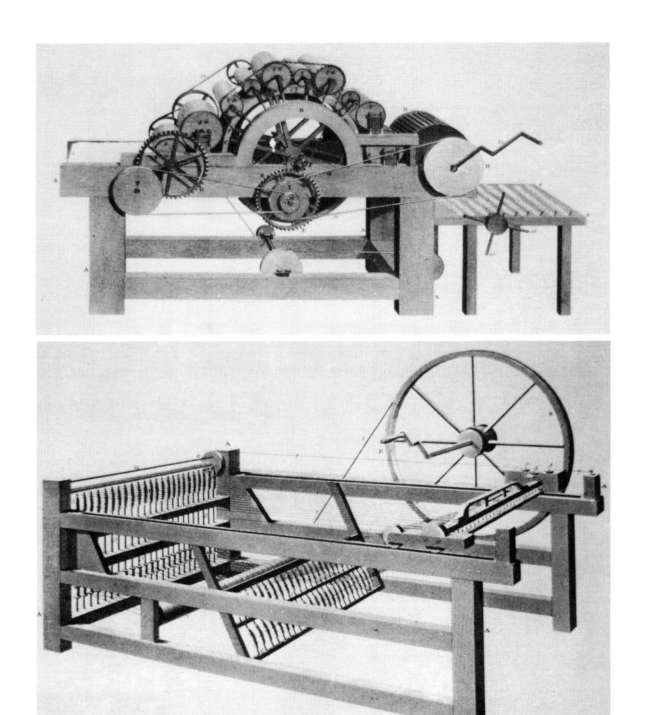

ABOVE: Carding engine and BELOW: spinning jenny.

On Friday the 13th day of December, 1794, at the Dwelling-House and Workshops of BRITON SALISBURY, Machine-Maker, a Bankrupt,

THREE SPINNING MACHINES, a Quantity of Oil, Wool, Yarn, Spindles, &c. together with his Stock in Trade, and Household Goods, a Rick of Hay, a Mare in Foal, a two yearling Colt, and two weanling Colts.

The sale to begin at eleven o'clock.

Precisely at two o'clock in the afternoon, will be Sold by Auction, the Lease of a Mill, with a Scribbling Machine, Carding Machine, and Slooping Machine, in full work; with sufficient room to add three other Machines; being held for a term of four years to come from Michaelmas last.

Particulars may be known by applying to Mr. M. Davies, Attorney, Warminster. [513

ENGINES for CARDING and SCRIBBLING WOOL, COTTON, &c. manufactured by Guppy and Armstrong, Bristol, warranted of the best seasoned timber, which entirely prevent the cylinder from warping, finished in the compleatest manner, with every late improvement by the most experienced workmen; having lately added many very experienced mechanics to their manufactory, they are enabled to serve the public with Engines at a very short notice.

☞ The cylinders may be made of deal, sycamore, beech or mahogany, which make a considerable difference in the price.

Clothiers may be supplied with warranted Cards of any dimensions, G. and A. having contracted with some of the best Yorkshire Card-makers for a regular supply. Also Tacks, Hammers, and Pincers, for nailing the cards. [220

To CLOTHIERS, &c.

MESSRS. POBJOY, MORGAN, ALLWOOD, and HARRIS, Cardmakers, Frome, Somerset, most respectfully inform the Manufacturers of Cloth, Cotton, &c. that they have (at great expence) procured compleat Machinery for manufacturing ENGINE-CARDS of every kind, on the Yorkshire plan. They have also engaged a person who is well acquainted with the method of making Cards in the North of England, to manage their machines.

They are encouraged to hope for the countenance and support of the manufacturers in general, as they are now enabled to supply them on the shortest notice, with Cards manufactured in the most approved manner, and at reduced prices.

Orders, directed to John Pobjoy and Co. Frome, will be faithfully executed. [147

LEFT: Spinning jenny at Courts Mill, Trowbridge c1900, now in the Science Museum, London. BELOW: Slubbing billy. RIGHT: Advertisements of early machinemakers, 1794–1795.

ABOVE: Gig mill and BELOW: shearing frame.

Wonderfully Improved

The spinning jenny was driven by the operator, who turned a wheel to make it perform its successive motions of drawing out, spinning, and winding on. Carding and scribbling machines, which needed continuous motion, could also be driven by human power. John Ford, the Frome maker, advertised in 1791 that his were 'made on such improved mechanical principles that even a boy may constantly work them', and the Trowbridge firm of John and Thomas Clark started in 1801 with a blind man turning their one engine. The work must have been unattractive, and a Frome maker in 1793 advertised 'a curious automaton for driving one or more carding engines without the aid of manual labour'. References to human power are naturally rare; it may have been quite commonly used but, for the operation of several machines, it was probably more economical to use a horse or donkey.

Horse-driven apparatus where the horse (s) walked round and round, or within a vertical wheel, was widely used, at least from the 16th century, for grinding malt or winding up buckets. A Salisbury fancy-cloth manufacturer, William Jesser, owned a fulling mill worked by a horse with a cog-wheel 18 ft in diameter, in 1784. If Anstie used carding machinery in his large building at Devizes from 1785 onwards, he may well have used horse-power. Joseph Phelps was using a horse mill at his workshops adjoining Westbury House in Bradford in 1794, and the horse was among the effects offered for sale. As there was only one horse Phelps may have been using a vertical wheel, like the one 36 ft in diameter offered for sale at Trowbridge in 1796. The horizontal kind enabled several horses to be used at once; one for four horses was for sale at Warminster in 1807, and in the same town a three-horse one,with an open wheel-house 23 ft in diameter, was offered in 1808. Other advertisements show horse-wheels were common. A horse-mill and workshops in the centre of Frome were claimed to be capable of making12–15 pieces in 1813, and a factory on the Green at Calne,which was driven by a horse-wheel as late as 1825, contained three scribbling and four carding engines, three tuckers, a wool mill, seven shearing frames, and a brushing machine.

Many clothiers already had workshops of considerable size adjoining their houses when machinery came. Others, like John Anstie, put up special buildings of formal design which look like small factories, though the term workshop was still generally used. A good example stood in Yerbury Street, Trowbridge, dated to 1793–6, and part of Silver Street Factory in the same town was built to be driven by horses in 1795. Another large workshop, which later expanded into a factory, stood beside the bridge at Chippenham. Others from before 1800 stand in Bradford, Rode, Frome, and Calne.

Investment in buildings and machinery must have been considerable. Only one set of bills for building a workshop has so far been found; it relates to a small building in Church Street, Westbury, standing in the garden behind a house, and only used for hand-worked machinery. It was built in 1823–4 and cost £520. Some of the larger workshops could well have cost £2,000. According to the stock books of J. & T. Clark of Trowbridge for 1804 onwards, a carding engine with a billy was worth about £90, and jennies from £6 to £9, depending on the number of spindles. Nevertheless, clothiers appear to have installed scribbling, carding and spinning machinery as a matter of course, and by 1800 the old methods of preparing yarn must have been obsolete.

Clothiers with more capital and enterprise quickly turned to water to drive scribbling and carding machinery, which it would do more cheaply and on a larger scale than horses. The first place where it is known with absolute certainty is Avoncliff Mill. In December 1791 a twelve-year-old boy 'who with many others younger as well as older was employed . . . in managing and working the late improved machines and engines for cloth making, and having inadvertently in his playtime put and buckled one part or end of a long strap of leather round his waist, the other end was taken hold of by a large upright piece of timber called the mainshaft, constantly going round, turning, and working the engines, whereby he was whirled round with great force, his body bruised, his limbs shattered and beaten off so that he was instantly killed'. This mill, which stood at the Westwood end of the great weir on the Avon, had been a fulling mill, and had presumably been extended to take machinery for the tenants, who were Moggridge and Joyce, a Bradford firm. When the site was to let in 1811, what was probably the original water–driven factory of c1790 had four floors and two wheels, one of which drove the machinery, the other four pairs of fulling stocks.

Several other water-driven factories may have preceded Avoncliff. At the upper one of two mill sites on the Twerton side of the Avon below Bath, there stood in 1787 a fulling mill, which also contained a gig, and nearby were workshops with jennies in them. It passed into the hands of Samuel Paul Bamford in 1790; in 1797 he had a factory of six floors insured for £1,500, millwright's work for £1,000, and machinery for £2,250. Bamford had a number of shearing frames when he went bankrupt in 1802, and it must have been these that caused trouble at Twerton in 1798. It is likely that the situation of Twerton, well away from the centre of the clothing district, appealed to a clothier who wished to have a wide range of machinery. Bamford was almost the only local clothier known to have boarded apprentices in the way familiar in northern textile industries: he advertised for 40–60 children over nine of both sexes in 1793, and the factory had an apprentice house in 1802. North Bradley parish apprenticed seven boys to him on one day in 1799.

It is possible there was an early water-driven factory at Keynsham. At Malmesbury the cloth trade had died out c1750, when the last clothier, Joseph Cullurne, moved to Melksham. In 1790 Francis Hill, a Bradford clothier, bought a corn mill near the bridge from Cullurne's family, and built the large factory still standing there. The date is not recorded, but Hill probably built it immediately after he had bought the site. In 1797 the report of an action between Hill and a Malmesbury innkeeper tells us that Hill, 'a man of great knowledge in the principles of mechanics, was early sensible of the advantages to be derived to the clothing business from the use of machinery, but finding it impossible to overcome the prejudice of the great body of workmen employed at Bradford, he erected considerable works at Malmesbury, where he had the advantage of water, but where the clothing business had not before been carried on'. He had simply to bring a few workpeople from Bradford under contract to instruct the locals.

An even more remote site was at Chard in south Somerset, some 40 miles outside the main clothing area. Some gentlemen of Wiltshire were said in 1797 to have set up a considerable manufacture there. This was probably the firm of J.R. and T. Clark, whose two water-driven factories, used to make superfine cloths and cassimeres, were offered for sale in 1812.

But there were early water-driven factories in the heartland of the industry as well. Westbury Leigh Mill was let to a partnership of John Waldron of Trowbridge and Thomas Luke Meech in 1790, and about the same time these partners took a lease of the nearby Bull's Mill. Another firm, which had both Trowbridge and Westbury partners, bought Bitham Mill at Westbury in 1791. All three sites must have been acquired for driving carding machinery.

To avoid trouble was an advantage but, even when carding and scribbling machinery were tolerated, it was not always easy to find a suitable site.

It had never been easy to build a water mill on a new site, for to do so would damage the rights of mills above and below. One new site from the pre-machinery period was Ladydown, on the Biss just below Trowbridge, where a fulling mill was built c1726. Normally, however, the water rights of an existing mill would have to be acquired by purchasing, and mills were valuable. In the rush for water-power from 1790 onwards many suitable ones continued either fulling or corn mills. On a short stretch of the powerful River Frome the fulling mills at Langham, Tellisford, Stowford, and Iford remained in use, while mills in the centre of Chippenham and Melksham, the latter converted entirely to corn as late as 1793, demonstrate the value of corn mills in a thickly-populated area.

Dunkirk Factory as it survived until a few years ago.

Factors now largely unknown to us might also have played a part: Lord Lansdowne, for instance, when refusing to let a Bradford clothier convert a mill near Calne, said that he approved of machinery, but could better defend its use if he did not thus profit. Other landowners may not have wanted factory hands near their game preserves. But many mills on large estates were held on life-leases, and so were outside the direct control of their owners. When Trowbridge partners John Hooper Taunton and Thomas Vine rebuilt Corsley Mill, part of the Longleat estate, as a factory in 1800, they did so as tenants of the lifeholder, who advanced them money and received £80 a year extra rent over the 14 years of their initial lease. This proved a burden which they could hardly afford, and they regretted the isolated position of a factory worth £100 a year more if it had been within a mile of Bradford or Trowbridge.

By 1800 machinery was certainly driven by water at 37 sites, and possibly over 40. Some of these represent little more than the fitting of a few scribbling or carding engines to existing or slightly extended fulling mills, but the great majority – well over 30 – were specially built structures of four, five, or six storeys. It had been possible to build some of them while retaining existing fulling or corn mills. At Freshford, two large wings were attached to the 16th century fulling mill by 1796, and at Beckington a four-storeyed building was attached to an existing corn mill c1794.

Generally, however, the new factory replaced an existing mill, though only a few new sites were found. John Waldron of Trowbridge bought the highest corn mill on the Biss, at Dilton, and so was able to build a factory above it, and Moggridge and Joyce moved from their rented mill at Avoncliff to a new factory on a small stream running down to the Frome near Freshford. Other small streams used for the first time were at Holt, West Woodlands near Frome, and Edward Street in Westbury. At Heytesbury, one small stream running into the Wylye was utilised by John Gale Everett, but William Marven Everett was able to build one on the main river, by having part deepened, so that a sufficient fall could be obtained without damage to other mills.

Like Waldron and Moggridge and Joyce, the builders of the new factories were mainly established firms. Abraham Lloyd Edridge and Uriah Tarrant moved out of Chippenham to Christian Malford and Avon, on the River Avon above the town. John Anstie from waterless Devizes bought the corn mill at Poulshot in 1791. At Westbury water was plentiful and seven sites were in use before 1800. In the upper Wylye valley enterprise came entirely from the Everett family for, besides the two mills at Heytesbury, they were using machinery at Horningsham and at Bull Mill, Crockerton. At Frome the Sheppards had a factory just outside the town at Rodden, and other early mills near it were at Friggle Street, Claybridge, West Woodlands and Hapsford. Jenkins and Green, the largest firm at Shepton Mallet, had a factory at Darshill. Near Salisbury only one factory was certainly built by 1800, at Burdensball, Wilton, on the site now occupied by the carpet factory.

Besides Moggridge and Joyce's new factory at Dunkirk near Freshford, another Bradford firm, Bush, Newton, and Bush, had factories at Freshford, Limpley Stoke, and Clifford's Mill near Beckington. Apart from Taunton and Vine's move to Corsley, no Trowbridge firm is certainly known to have turned to water power at an early date, though the older part of the Stone Mill still standing in the town probably dates from before 1800. At Staverton, the largest water-driven factory in the whole area was built in 1800 by Bradford clothier John Jones.

By that time the introduction of scribbling, carding, and spinning machinery had been accomplished without much tribulation, and the idea of factory work was familiar throughout the clothing region, either in extensive workshop or water-driven factory conditions. This easy transition was eased by a period of prosperity. Exports of Spanish cloth and cassimere rose from £61,000 in 1796 to over £300,000 in 1800, and much of this was made in the west, though Gloucestershire was by now successfully making fine cassimeres and cutting into our area's previous monopoly. Gloucestershire clothiers were able to use the gig-mill for raising, which did the work better and more cheaply. All the lower parts of the western trade, those which used English wool, now lay at the mercy of Yorkshire; there carding and spinning machinery had been generally introduced a few years earlier, and the fly-shuttle had been used for weaving since the 1780s. An attempt to introduce it at Trowbridge in 1792 led to a riot, and a weaver who had used it in the north was forced to give it up at Freshford in 1800. The only example of early local use was at Malmesbury, where Francis Hill had 50 or 60 at his factory by 1803. By then it was widely used in Gloucestershire.

Yorkshire also scored over the west by using a considerable amount of steam power in addition to the ample water power of the Pennine slopes. Some of this was in the form of atmospheric engines of Savery or Newcomen type, which were applied to pump water back into the mill pond, so that it could pass over the wheel again. The excessive coal consumption of such engines would have made this prohibitive, for cost of coal was the crucial factor, and that cost was determined by distance from the pit. It is true that Frome was only six miles from the nearest pits, but it was comparatively well-supplied with water power: Trowbridge stood most in need of steam power, for the Biss is not fast-flowing nor copious since it runs through flattish country, but 10 miles of hilly country lay between the town and the nearest pit.

Apart from John Anstie, who thought of using an engine at Bristol in 1782, the first Wiltshire clothier known to have considered steam power was Henry Wansey of Salisbury. He enquired after an engine to drive carding machinery in 1791, but found the 5 hp one suggested by Boulton and Watt too large. Carriage of coal to Salisbury would certainly have been expensive. Boulton and Watt received several more enquiries from Warminster, Trowbridge, and Bradford between 1796 and 1800, but capital outlay and coal consumption were too great, compared to existing horse power.

Western clothiers then thought themselves at a disadvantage compared with Yorkshire. The circular from a Trowbridge clothier in 1798, which showed a loss on making a superfine broadcloth, was meant as a complaint about the high price of wool, but even if it was unduly pessimistic it shows how narrow margins could be. Whether he scribbled by hand or machine, he would have saved a lot if he could have raised and sheared by machine. William Jenkins of Shepton Mallet gave evidence to Parliament in 1800 about the decline of the coarse trade in his own town, Westbury and Warminster. Jenkins was unable to use the gig and the shearing frame, and had had some buildings burnt in 1799 when he was building a mill to scribble. He blamed the workpeople for the removal of the coarse trade to the north.

Luccombe Mill, Bratton.

The attack on Jenkins's mill was probably because it was suspected he would instal finishing machinery. He was given military protection, as were the clothiers at Twerton in 1798, when a mob of shearmen and others from Bradford, Trowbridge, Frome and Beckington intended to destroy both Bamford's factory and that of Collicott and Co on the opposite side of the river. It must have been shortly after this that detachments of troops were kept at the factories at Christian Malford and Avon, to protect the gig-mills and shearing frames. Hill was also using gig-mills at Malmesbury. Like Twerton, these factories were well away from the central area. Clothiers there, although aware that Gloucestershire was gaining ground by the free use of the gig, hardly dared introduce it. William Sheppard of Frome told the Parliamentary enquiry of 1802–3 that the preference given to Gloucestershire cloths was so great, that he had to send all his broad cloths there to be gigged, by which they were 'wonderfully improved'. He even accepted large orders for cloth to be delivered immediately after milling, and it is known that some factors arranged for dressing to be done in London. Not all clothiers agreed with Sheppard's judgement on the gig, for two from Chippenham said that cloth sent to Twerton had been strained as a result.

The gig first appeared in the main clothing area in 1802, at Warminster and at John Jones's new factory at Staverton. Jones had until then been sending his cloths to Wotton-under-Edge. The immediate result was that the great majority of shearmen stopped work, saying they would not work after the gig. At Frome, William Sheppard offered his men constant work at 14s a week, while Jones made a series of concessions which guaranteed work for all unemployed shearmen in Bradford parish, (where he lived, though his factory was in Trowbridge parish), and undertook that he would not shear by machine while any were unemployed, and would not do work for other manufacturers. The men refused, saying that shearmen all over Great Britain were resolved not to work after machines.

The local shearmen appear to have been organised in some way as early as 1788, when the journeymen clothworkers of Bradford were convicted of conspiring to establish innovations in their trade, and to prevent their masters from taking apprentices. Trouble there recurred in 1791, when it became customary to make new entrants pay a large fine before working. This was also prevalent at Shepton Mallet, where the clothiers requested in 1790 that only the customary fee of 1s should be taken. At Bradford the clothiers and master clothworkers advertised that they were determined to stop this oppressive combination. There were early-18th century Acts directed against combinations in the woollen industry; in 1799 and 1800 two Acts made combinations of workpeople illegal in general.

In spite of them, the shearmen were highly organised. In June 1802 a Warminster lawyer reported to the government that the shearmen had not worked for many weeks, and were supporting one another through secret combinations: 'they have at present no visible means of any livelihood, and there is good reason to think they are supported and encouraged by contributions from many of the innkeepers and other inhabitants . . .' Many outrages had been committed in and around Warminster.

A few weeks later John Jones of Staverton asked if he would be justified in arresting the committee of 13 men, who ran the Trowbridge shearmen's union, and seizing their books and papers. They were raising a countrywide subscription to support the men not working, and issued a union card which entitled its holder to relief. There were regular contacts with Yorkshire shearmen. Jones's own workpeople were leaving under threat of attack, and he was afraid he would have to stop the factory. He too reported many outrages, and attacks were made on the factory in which firearms were used. It is to the credit of the Joneses, father and son, that they tried, apparently unsuccessfully, to prevent the government from prosecuting the delegation of seven men who discussed the matter with them for conspiracy, since they had been promised immunity. At Frome too, Sheppards reported that their workpeople had stood by them until 'intimidated by the harsh threats of the multitude. They are for the most part *now sworn* to secrecy and *dare* not return. The extent of this league cannot be fathomed . . .'

In July 1802 the Trowbridge shearmen burnt two properties belonging to Francis Naish, who had an extensive trade in fancy waistcoatings. One was his own workshop in Trowbridge, the other the mill at Littleton near Semington, which he had let to Ralph Heath, and in which shearing frames were installed. The men were armed and had blacked their faces. A reward of £50 was offered for the apprehension of a man who was 'middle sized, black eyes, thin face, teeth large in front and wide apart, sharp nose, black hair tied behind, and dressed in a blue jacket'. Thomas Hilliker, a youth of 19, was taken; he admitted that he was a member of the shearmen's club and had taken an oath, and told the magistrates that the committee met on Wednesdays. An attempt to arrest the committee was bungled, but James May, its clerk, was taken, and identified by a printer as the man who had ordered the rules and tickets to be printed. The ticket was copied from one which had the word *Leeds* at the bottom. May and four other committee men were subsequently charged with administering an unlawful oath, but acquitted because, it was alleged, the principal witness against them had been tampered with.

Greenland Upper Mill, Bradford.

In August the Wiltshire and Somerset clothiers issued a statement, promising to find work for all whose jobs were replaced by machines, at reasonable wages. But the government agent, James Read, reported that not a single shearman was at work at Staverton, and that at Warminster the clothiers were using shearing frames because none would work after the gigs. Read took an active part: 'Two or more Justices meet daily at one or other of the manufacturing towns', he wrote, 'and as the Combination Act affords a very convenient pretext for summoning and examining on oath any suspected persons, I have continually some before them. It answers the double purpose of keeping the magistrates at their post and of alarming the disaffected'. In October he reported that the shearmen's wives were becoming impatient, and that the Warminster shearmen were beginning to go back to work. He sensibly tried to influence the clothiers to take the men back without resentment, and to employ all that would return.

Thomas Hilliker was tried at the Lent Assize in 1803, found guilty, and executed. His body was brought back to Trowbridge and buried in the churchyard; the claim that he was innocent and died because he refused to implicate the real culprits is not made in any near-contemporary source. The whole episode of violence in 1802–3 retarded the general introduction of finishing machinery for some years, though there is no evidence that it was withdrawn from places where it was in use. The general opinion was that many of the smaller clothiers and master shearmen who worked on commission were quite content to do without it. Intermittent violence occurred, probably where clothiers continued to use it or tried to introduce it. At Staverton the younger John Jones was shot in the face as he rode home from the factory in 1807, and in that year an attempt

79

was made to burn Kingston Mill at Bradford, then newly built. The German traveller Nemnich, who wrote an account of a journey through the clothing area in 1807, found that the clothiers warned him not to speak of machinery in the presence of the workpeople. Jones would not let him into Staverton at all, but told him that if the building was not there he would never undertake it again.

When Nemnich came, trade was brisk, and the demand for cassimeres was so great that clothiers were at their wits' end to fulfil orders. At Salisbury he was told of the great improvements in the making of flannels by the use of Spanish and other fine wool and by the use of machinery for spinning. Few flannels were dyed in Salisbury, but went to other places in Wiltshire and Somerset or, if scarlet was required, to Stroud. Wilton was now chiefly noted for carpets, but there were also three large manufacturers of cassimeres. Devizes was still making serges, but they were now less good than they had been 50 years earlier. Various patterned cassimeres and other fashion goods were also made there, a fact borne out by the one surviving pattern book of a Devizes clothier, which consists entirely of striped and mottled cloths.

The superfine broadcloth and cassimere manufacture was the staple of all the west Wiltshire towns from Chippenham and Corsham down to Warminster. At Frome only Sheppards made cloth of that type; the standard product of that town, Shepton Mallet and the villages around was Second Cloth.

The period of generally good trade continued until the end of the war in 1815, and encouraged investment. Some clothiers still built workshops, which were presumably driven by horses, or in which they only used spinning jennies. Firmly dated examples are of 1816 from Trowbridge and Great Hinton, and c1818 at Seend. The builder of the Seend ones certainly used them for spinning, and did his scribbling and carding at the mill at Bulkington. Jones told the 1803 enquiry that he scribbled for some 'inferior manufacturers', and obviously considerable trades could be carried on without the use of a full-sized factory. John and Thomas Clark, the Trowbridge partnership begun in 1801, were making 300 cloths a year by 1805, and nearly 1,200 by 1813, using workshops in Duke Street which by 1813 contained only carding and spinning machinery.

The search for available sites with water was still continuing, and a number of new factories appeared in the early years of the century. At Bradford, four large ones on the upper side of the bridge, which used the power derived from the weir at Greenland, were built c1804–8. At Bratton, Thomas Jarvis converted a large corn mill for machinery c1805, and built two more factories on the same stream in 1807 and 1809. The two water-driven factories at Rode are first heard of about the same time, and other examples come from Wellhead at Westbury and Upton Lovell, both 1807, and Westbury Town Mill, 1812. At late as 1818 a Bradford clothier converted a paper mill at Slaughterford. The last water-driven factory to be built was in a extraordinary situation at Tisbury, far to the south of the clothing district. It was supplied by the great ornamental lake at Fonthill, and was large, with two buildings of six and five storeys. It was completed in 1827 and run for two years by the nephew of the eccentric Mr Farquhar, who owned the Fonhill estate. It was then sold for £12,000, having cost £38,000 to build, and the machinery was sold in 1830. No more is known of it.

At Salisbury itself small factories were attached to the fulling mill at West Harnham and the corn mill at Fisherton, and machinery was driven by water at Milford, Barford St Martin, and Quidhampton. None of these was large concerns, and it is clear that the trade in and around the city was insufficient to warrant much investment, probably owing to the competition of flannels made in the north. The stocks of several clothiers were sold: William Hutchins of Milford Street and Mr Mitchell of the same street, both in 1807, each had carding and spinning machinery, while in March 1809 two businesses, both said to be old-established and extensive with adequate machinery, were advertised in the same paper. One was certainly the firm of Hinxman, Hussey and Co, some of whose equipment was sold the next year. It was no exaggeration to call it a large trade, for Henry Hinxman's share in it was worth over £10,000 in 1805, and his profit on his capital between 1796 and 1805, apart from one disastrous year of 1798, was generally between six and ten per cent. In 1806–7, however, it fell to under four, and things may have been worse by 1809.

Salisbury's trade did not die for another 40 years. Machinery was destroyed in the 1830 Labourers' Revolt riots at the small factories at Barford St Martin (then apparently used for silk manufacture), Quidhampton, Milford, and Figheldean, and none was re-started. Three clothiers remained in 1844 of whom one, Alexander Minty, was using West Harnham Mill to make yarn for sale. By 1848 nothing remained in the city. At Wilton, however, Crow Lane Mill, where machinery was also destroyed in 1830, was set up again, and used by William Naish, woollen cord manufacturer. He later turned over to making felt, and the mill is still used by E.V. Naish and Co in this trade.

Quemerford Mill, Calne, a water-driven factory with steam power added.

In the reminder of the area, a new impetus to investment was the completion in April 1805 of the Somerset Coal Canal, which ran from the Kennet and Avon Canal near Limpley Stoke to the pits near Radstock. This was of the greatest advantage to Bradford and Trowbridge. Devizes, Melksham, Chippenham, and Calne also had direct water transport, although their greater distance added to cost. Westbury gained, in that coal could be brought to Bradford or Hilperton Marsh Wharves, and then hauled over fairly level roads. Frome got no advantage at all. It is significant that the first steam engine was fitted at Trowbridge, in June 1805. The firm, Cooper and Son of Duke Street, had been using workshops which must have been horse-driven for some years. They enquired of Boulton and Watt for the prices of small engines in 1802 and 1804, but presumably rejected the idea of fitting one on the grounds of fuel cost.

The Cooper engine was of only 6 hp, and was probably fitted in the existing buildings. Boulton and Watt tended to advise their clients against fitting small engines, and it may be that clothiers went elsewhere. There was, for instance, a 3 hp engine at Woolley near Bradford which was probably erected c1808 (certainly by 1811), and a small one drove workshops at Whitehill in the town in 1818. Several others are known at Trowbridge and Chippenham. The maker of one of these small engines was Mr Woods of Oxford, who supplied a 4 or 5 hp engine to Courtney and Co in Crane Street, Salisbury, c1808. When they were bankrupt, a Salisbury millwright bought it and put it up for sale, pointing out that it could easily be moved back to the west of the county by return carriage of coal waggons.

Other early buyers of engines were owners of water-driven factories, who were often unable to run them continuously because water was short, or because the rivers were in flood. Thomas Jarvis of Bratton bought a 6 hp Boulton and Watt engine when he was building a factory on a new site at Bratton in 1807, though he also had a wheel there. Factories on small streams were quick to add steam power, so that Adderwell at Frome and Dunkirk at Freshford both had them by 1810. By the 1820s few water-factories of any size were without a steam engine, though one, Scutt's Bridge at Rode, worked solely by water-power until it closed c1904.

From fitting engines to workshops and water-factories, it was only a short step to building factories specially to be driven by steam. Angel Mill at Westbury was begun in March 1806, and its size indicates clearly that it was built to be steam-powered. Boulton and Watt supplied two engines to Bradford in 1807, one to a large factory built by Saunders and Fanner (on the site of the present Abbey Mill). South Parade Factory at Frome dates from the same year, and Bridge Mill at Trowbridge was built in 1808. From then on there were regular additions until the late 1820s. They were almost all in the towns, though one was built at Chapmanslade in 1814, and another of unknown date in Rode.

The Boulton and Watt archives show that about 27 engines were certainly erected in our area between 1805 and 1828. Others of their make may have been used, for engines were moved, and they themselves would occasionally offer a second-hand one. When J. and T. Clark of Trowbridge ordered a 10 hp engine in 1814 (at a total cost of £984, including carriage and erection), Boulton and Watt sent George Haden, one of their engine fitters, to Trowbridge, and he decided to set up an independent business. He came to live in the town in 1816, acting partly as a Boulton and Watt agent and partly as a general millwright. His firm still exists as an international heating and ventilating concern, and from quite early in its history that part of the business was important. But it made a small engine for George Wansey of Warminster as early as 1824, and in the 1830s supplied several to factories at Trowbridge and Bratton. Their 50 hp engine at Cradle Bridge Mill, Trowbridge, was one of the largest in the area.

Hadens had a millwrighting business which took them all over the clothing area and into Gloucestershire as well, and involved work on water wheels, including erection, as well as on engines and machinery. There were several other firms in the same field. Wheelers of Rode supplied fulling stocks to one of the largest Yorkshire factories as early as 1793, and Thomas Mines of Fisherton near Salisbury claimed that his water wheels were made on proper scientific principles in 1810. Wastfields of Bradford were also noted makers of water-wheels. Nor did Hadens have a monopoly in locally made steam engines. John Dyer, a Trowbridge engineer, fitted an engine of his own make to Silver Street Mill in 1811, and made ten others up to 1816. The largest, of 12 hp, fitted to Upper Greenland Mill at Bradford, cost £600, notably cheaper than a comparable Boulton and Watt engine. Dyer's son preserved the story that James Watt visited Trowbridge and admired the ingenuity of one of his father's engines, telling George Haden not to interfere with his business. Boulton and Watt's reputation was great, however, and several factory-owners tried to persuade them to 'correct' engines they had bought from other makers, usually without success.

Investment continued in buildings and machinery even when it was not possible to use a full range of machinery at many places. Gig-mills and shearing frames continued in use at the places where they had caused troubles in the earlier years of the century: there were three gigs and 42 frames at Staverton in 1813. By that time they are certainly known to have been used at Calne, Freshford and Stony Littleton, the last a remote situation. At Trowbridge, however, Bridge Mill contained no finishing machinery when its contents were sold in 1811, nor did a smaller factory at Woolley, Bradford, in the same year. J. and T. Clark of Trowbridge had none until 1816, when they bought 11 shearing frames from Harmer of Sheffield at a cost, including carriage, of £399. In 1817 an attempt was made to set John Clark's house on fire because he was using gigs. Another

Trowbridge factory had eight gigs in 1816, and clearly finishing machinery was generally tolerated, if not liked, by about 1820. The burning down of South Parade Factory at Frome in 1821 was the work of an unknown incendiary.

The fly-shuttle caused disturbances at Bradford and Chippenham in 1816, and in 1822 in the area round Frome. Sheppards, the largest firm in Frome, refused to give out work to weavers who used the double loom, which was thought to do less uniform work, and they seem to have won their point, though it is not known if the fly-shuttle was ever completely adopted. Most weaving was still done at the weavers' houses. Weaving shops at the clothiers' houses had appeared in the 1780s, when the popularity of fancy cassimeres encouraged clothiers to set them up, and this caused resentment. The owners of factories at Malmesbury and Christian Malford had weaving shops in 1803 because, they said, there were no weavers in the neighbourhood, but Jones at Staverton told the commissioners that he had no intention of setting one up, as he would need a four-storeyed building for the 100 broad looms he needed. In spite of this there was a weaving shop for 40 spring looms at his factory in 1813.

Another water mill, later steam powered: Upton Lovell Mill.

The building of factories, especially those of size and visual impact such as Staverton, must have been striking, but no contemporary commented on it, nor on the startling change which working in factory conditions had on the lives of so many people. Once clothiers had invested in a factory and power, they wanted to run fairly long hours when trade was good. In 1816 most factories were running 10 or 11 hours a day, with two hours above this allowed for meals, so that they started at six and finished at six or seven. On Saturdays they finished at two.

This is clear from the local answers to a Parliamentary enquiry into the state of children in factories. John Bush, a Bradford solicitor, analysed the employees of 33 principal firms by sex, age, and ability to read or write. The variation in numbers employed by firms is so great (321 to 35) that it seems likely that some included out-workers in their replies and some did not. Most employed some children under ten years old, and seven was regarded as a usual starting age. A good proportion of under-tens could read; presumably they had learnt at Sunday schools. Certificates from the medical men in Bradford, Trowbridge, and Westbury said that the factory children were as healthy as those in other occupations.

The firms mentioned in Bush's table were at Bradford (9), Staverton, Holt, Avoncliff, Trowbridge (7), Heytesbury (2), Westbury (3), Bratton, Chippenham (2), Calne, Twerton, Frome, Freshford (2), and Rode. As a picture of the industry when it was approaching its greatest extent it is inadequate, though it certainly included all the largest firms. After 1820 few new factories were built, and some began to fall out of use or to be converted.

A tentative analysis of the industry c1820 shows there were some 75 factories of considerable size, in an area which was bounded by Malmesbury, Calstone near Calne, Devizes, Upton Lovell, the upper reaches of the River Frome, Shepton Mallet, and Twerton. Of these some 28 had been built to be driven by steam, 13 were water-factories which had had steam engines added, and the remaining 35 were probably driven by water alone. Almost all were occupied by firms which carried out all the processes then found in factories, *ie* yarn manufacture and finishing, for their own trade. Some may have been under-used, for remarks made later about Malmesbury and Christian Malford suggest that none of the four factories there worked to capacity.

Of these factories, 14 were in Trowbridge, all steam-driven, and nine in Bradford, of which eight had steam power either alone or added to powerful wheels. In the second rank came Frome and Westbury, each with seven factories, and with four and one steam engines respectively. The history of individual factories in Shepton Mallet is obscure, and sizeable ones may not have numbered more than three at this time. Only one steam-driven factory is known to have existed there, and that may not have worked after 1814. There were three factories at Twerton, one with an engine, and three at Chippenham. The others were scattered through the area in ones and twos; the formerly important town of Melksham had only two, and there was one each at Devizes and Calne. No factory of size had appeared at Warminster, nor at Salisbury.

To these we must add 40 or more smaller factories, many of which probably had only scribbling and carding machinery, though at least one, at Calstone near Calne, contained only fulling stocks, gig mills, and shearing frames. Few of these buildings survive, but typical examples in terms of size would be the mill near the bridge at Rode, and those at Lullington and Corsley. Some mills of this size were used by clothiers in association with workshops. At Calne the firm of Viveash and Co had a complete range of machinery, partly at Sprays Mill at Calstone, and partly in the town, and William Gaisford of Seend did his scribbling, carding, and slubbing at Bulkington. Clothiers from Frome used mills on the River Frome above the town, and in the Spring Gardens and Nunney areas in the same way. Egford Mill near Whatley was probably typical, using a 4 hp wheel, and employing 13 hands in 1838. The remnants of the industry in and around Salisbury, where Minty employed 15 hands at West Harnham in 1838, would have been on the same scale. The country mills were all water-powered; in the towns there were certainly some factories of comparable size driven by small steam engines, such as the ones at Bradford, Trowbridge and Chippenham.

There were still many firms without factory accommodation. In 1822 there were 29 firms at Trowbridge, about half of which had no factories of their own. In some cases they are known to have occupied workshops, and no doubt all did so to some extent. Judging by the rating of stock-in-trade, by no means all these clothiers were small. Thomas Stillman, for instance, was rated as highly as the owners of medium-sized factories in the town, and is known to have carried on his business from workshops in the Conigre. Clothiers without factories could also get work done on commission by other firms, or at country mills which specialised in it.

In Trowbridge there were also two factories run by Strang and Webber, who described themselves as 'millowners and workers of steam engines'. In their factories they would let space for clothiers to place their own machines, and connect them to the shafting driven by the factory engine, which was guaranteed to work for set numbers of hours. They also had some machinery of their own hired out with power supply. This is the only firm known to have exploited whole factories, but other clothiers may have let some machinery. In 1839 John Tucker, 'undertaker in the clothing manufacture' had a carding engine and a billy in William Stancomb's factory in Trowbridge.

Although many factories now contained fulling stocks and included dyehouses, some factory clothiers still preferred to have these processes done by specialists, who also got custom from the workshop clothiers. Some 20 mills which only did fulling were at work, almost all driven by water, though Ladydown Mill near Trowbridge had a steam engine by 1828. Custom dyehouses were still to be found, at Trowbridge (where there were four), Bradford, Rode, Frome, and Corsley.)

An early steam-driven factory: former Abbey Mill, Bradford, c1807.

LEFT: New Park Street, Devizes, workshops dated 1785. RIGHT: The Green, Calne, workshops. BELOW: Silver Street Factory, Trowbridge, which developed from workshops built 1795 – the range to the left of the chimney.

LEFT: Willow Vale, Frome, workshops. RIGHT: An early water-driven factory on the Avon below Bath: Twerton Upper (and see over). BELOW: Weavers' Cottages, Seend – formerly and more aptly named Factory Row, built as workshops 1818, and designed so that they would easily convert to houses.

ABOVE: Twerton Lower and BELOW: Weston – both on the Avon, both
waterdriven.

ABOVE: Avon Mill, Malmesbury: the earlier part, c1790, to the left of the
archway, the remainder built by 1803. BELOW: Westbury Leigh Mill, 1873.
(WRO)

ABOVE: Freshford Mill, early 19th century: the 16th-century fulling mill in front of the chimney. (CDL)
CENTRE: Bull Mill, Crockerton. LEFT: Boyers Mill, Westbury Leigh, c1797. RIGHT: Token issued by
Moggridge and Joyce of Dunkirk, Freshford, 1795 – note the die-maker's error.

ABOVE LEFT: Staverton Factory, as re-instated after the fire of 1824. (WRO)
RIGHT: Trowbridge Shearmen's Union card, 1802. BELOW LEFT:
John Cooper of Trowbridge, who first introduced steam power into the
area. RIGHT: Kingston Mill, Bradford, on a bill-heading of 1818.

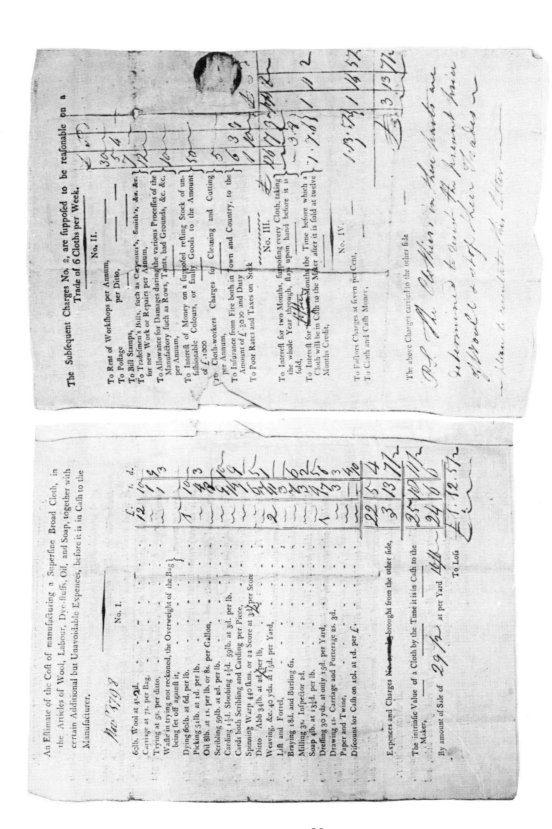

Circular issued by a Trowbridge clothier about costing, 1798.

ABOVE: The Avon at Bradford, harnessed to drive four factories. (WRO)
LEFT: Water-driven factories with steam power added: Twerton Upper Mill
and RIGHT: Stone Mill, Trowbridge.

93

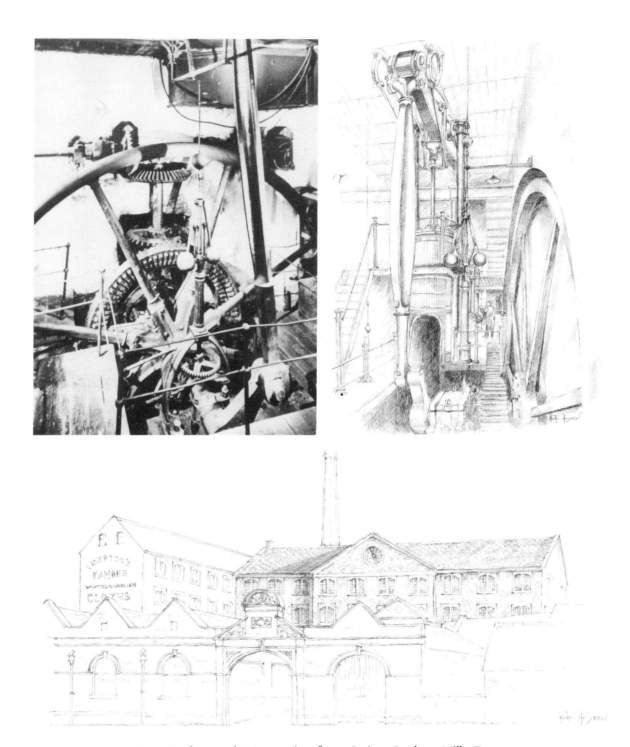

LEFT: Boulton and Watt engine from Spring Gardens Mill, Frome, afterwards at Chard. (FM) RIGHT: Engine at Bitham Mill, Westbury, 1829–1939. Early steam-driven factory at BELOW: Angel Mill, Westbury, 1806.

ABOVE: Bridge Mill, Trowbridge, c1808 and BELOW: Courts Mill, Trowbridge, 1812, both steam-driven.

ABOVE: Courts Mill, Trowbridge, photographed before demolition, 1968: note the beam engine house. BELOW: Bridge Factory, Chippenham.

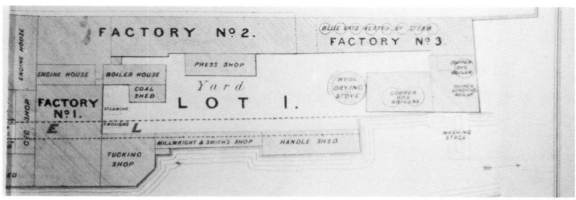

Waterford Factory, Chippenham, plan, (WRO) and photograph c1900.
(CM)

ABOVE: Model of the Boulton and Watt engine fitted to J. and T. Clark's
factory at Trowbridge by George Haden, 1814. BELOW: Model of Haden's
patent gigmill. (TM)

Hard Times

The end of the war in 1815 led to depression in some sectors; uniform cloth commissioned for the Austrian army from Wanseys of Warminster never found a market, and supplied the family with curtains and dress lengths for many years. Chippenham, Melksham, and Warminster suffered from depression in 1816 so that subscriptions had to be raised for the poor. But in 1817 there was scarcely a weaver not working in Bradford and Trowbridge, and a traveller for Joyce, Cooper and Co of Staverton said that he never remembered money more plentiful or trade more brisk. Trowbridge in particular prospered. In 1814 the sale of the site of the mediaeval castle brought a long stretch of riverside on to the market, and several steam-driven factories were built. The population grew from 6,075 to 9,545 between 1811 and 1821, making it the largest town in Wiltshire; 500 new houses were built, many of the new streets showing an interesting alternation between three-storeyed houses intended to provide space for domestic work, and two storeyed ones for factory workers. Bradford and Frome grew as well, though at only half the rate. In contrast Chippenham and Salisbury showed little growth.

The 1820s were variable. In 1820 work at Trowbridge was so short that people hauled coal from the Radstock pits yoked together like oxen, but in 1822 factories were working day and night. In 1826, 4000 people depended on the parish or charity for their livelihood; then came two better years, and worse distress than ever in 1829. Yet the firm of J. and T. Clark increased its capital from £10,929 in 1815 to £59,258 in 1825, and invested in much scribbling, carding, spinning and finishing machinery. Between 1820 and 1825 it made profits of between 16 and 22 per cent, except for 1823. That year the number of cloths was static, but profit was under 2 per cent. John Stancomb built the extensive Castle Factory in 1828. In the whole decade there were nine bankruptcies in the town, but only two were of factory clothiers – Thomas Deacon at Studley Mill in 1825, and Coopers of Duke Street a year later.

At Bradford three firms which occupied factories stopped in the 1820s – Stoddart and Co of Greenland Middle Mill, Hopkins and Howard of Kingston Mill, and Samuel Hart and Co at Church Street and Woolley. None of these factories was occupied again for some years, and the one at Woolley is not heard of again. Shepton Mallet and Frome suffered more severely than the Wiltshire towns, because there Yorkshire competition was most damaging.

It was said in 1828 that the second and livery clothiers made the mistake of using all English wool for these cloths, whereas Yorkshire had discovered that better materials could be produced from foreign or mixed foreign and English wools. There were 12 bankruptcies at Frome in 1823–4, all apparently of non-factory clothiers, and only one factory is known to have stopped. This was the small one at Leonard's Mill below the town, which was put up for sale on the death of the clothier in 1828, and not heard of again. On the other hand, Richard Brittain built a steam-driven factory at Vallis Way in 1823. At Shepton William Gaite, who occupied two factories at Darshill, was bankrupt in 1824. The 1830 *Directory* refers to extreme depression in the town, though ten firms remained. By then the largest firm at Shepton was Nalder and Hardisty, silk throwsters and silk, gros de Naples and crêpe manufactures, who were occupying four former woollen mills by 1833.

Silk throwing was established as a factory industry near Bruton. A manufacturer named Hoddinott advertised for from 100 to 200 girls between 8 and 12 years old as apprentices in 1812, but his steam-powered factory at Milton between Bruton and Shepton Mallet was up for sale a year later. A silk and crêpe manufacturer built a sizeable factory at Merchant's Barton in Frome in 1823, and in the 1820s empty woollen mills at Chippenham, Devizes, Batheaston, and Crockerton were all converted for this trade. The conversion of Chapp's Mill at Slaughterford in 1827 to a paper mill marked the end of the woollen industry in the By Brook valley, and the trade at Devizes ceased when Waylen's steam-driven factory in Northgate Street stopped work c1830. The two mills at Calstone near Calne stopped in 1825 and 1830, and Anstie's former scribbling mill at Poulshot was given up in 1828.

In such difficult times wages both for weavers and factory workers fell, as Cobbett was told in 1826, when he found some Bradford factory hands who had walked all the way to Heytesbury to gather nuts. After the riots against spring looms and reduced wages in 1822, the government was greatly alarmed by evidence of organised activities to get a return to the former price for weaving. Weavers who accepted the lower wages were intimidated, and several men were sent to prison for neglecting their work. The Frome justices, at the instance of the clothiers, took high-handed action to recover materials from the houses of weavers on strike; warrants which were not strictly legal were issued and, when they were resisted, doors were broken down and goods taken by force. These proceedings earned a stern warning from Peel, then Home Secretary, but a troop of cavalry was still needed in 1824 to keep order in the town. The Frome weavers issued a well-presented statement, and started a Society for the Suppression of Truck, which was to meet regularly at the Unicorn Inn with the permission of the magistrates.

The distress of 1829 occurred in the second half of the year, so it was while the comparative prosperity of 1828 still existed that a union club modelled on those in Yorkshire appeared in the area. It aimed to abolish truck and to improve wages, acting in concert throughout the western and northern textile regions. A large proportion of workpeople joined and were admitted by the taking of ceremonial oaths, and support came from tradespeople who were afraid of losing custom. 'Prayer meetings were held on its behalf, and the principal members walked in solemn procession, headed by one of their number apparelled in the robes of a bishop' wrote W.H. Tucker of Trowbridge. The union attempted to gain its objects by means of selective striking, and chose Matravers and Overbury of Westbury for its first action. The Westbury strikers were supported by Trowbridge members with 8s a week each, amounting to over £200 a week but, by the end of April, after being out for eight or nine weeks, payments had ceased and they were in 'a dreadful state of privation'. The firm refused to re-employ, and one man sold a piece of cloth for 4s in Westbury market which he said he had received in lieu of 6s 6d wages.

The strike was probably hopeless even in good times, but the possibility of further action disappeared with the intense distress of 1829–30. In Frome it was said that 5,000 people were unemployed, and at Trowbridge a government inspector said he had never encountered 'such a scene of rags and ghastly faces'. Several newspapers published a statement that 70 mills in the western wool area were to let but, if true, it must have related to the serge-manufacturing area further west, as well as to our area and Gloucestershire.

Trowbridge's difficulties were partly owing to a fall in the US export trade of cassimeres, when the tariff was raised in 1828. It was not reduced until 1835, but Trowbridge, and indeed the whole area, showed an improvement soon after 1830, and by 1833 a Bradford clothier could say that trade had never been better. Clarks of Trowbridge made 9½ per cent profit in 1832 and 14 per cent in 1833. But at the end of 1836 a national depression began which lasted until 1842, and the woollen industry suffered thereby.

The depression was blamed on the Corn Laws by many clothiers, who contended that, with free trade, the Americans would buy cloth and pay in corn. At a meeting in 1842, some chilling facts were revealed. At Bradford, out of 19 manufacturers active in 1820, nine had gone bankrupt, and eight declined business. A factory let for £1,200 in 1820 was now occupied for £300, and another formerly let for £300 was now partly used at £60. Out of 462 looms in the Bradford area, only 11 were fully at work, and 135 partly so.

At Westbury 354 out of 676 looms were unemployed, and the weavers could only earn 6 or 7s a week. The pawnshops were flourishing because of trade with 'the middle classes', the poor having long ago pledged all they had. At Melksham 32 looms at factories were in full work, but only 79 out of 168 at weavers' houses were used. Trowbridge clothiers also complained at the decline of exports compared with earlier times, but nothing specific was said about the town, and the *Bath Chronicle* subsequently published a query evidently supplied by a protectionist clothier – if the Corn Laws had caused the difficulties, why had Trowbridge gone up as fast as Bradford had gone down?

Bradford: steam-driven factories in Church Street and Mason's Lane from a photograph of c1860.

The depressions saw the end of the trade in the Salisbury area, Warminster, and Shepton Mallet, The largest mill near Calne, at Quemerford, stopped in 1841, and only one small business remained. One of the two large factories at Heytesbury was sold up in 1831, and in Bath the conversion of Bathwick Mill to corn alone in 1839 marked the end of the industry in the city centre. The depression of 1838–42 had a particularly severe effect in Bradford, partly owing to the failure of Hobhouse's Bank at Bath, which ruined itself by allowing credit to Cooper and Co of Staverton and Saunders and Co of Greenland Lower Mill at Bradford and Limpley Stoke Mill, both of which went bankrupt. Samuel Pitman at Kingston Mill, William Halwey at Bull Pit; Yerbury, Edmunds and Co at Greenland Upper Mill, and Samuel Mundy and Co all stopped trading, and the latter's factory adjoining the Chantry was pulled down. Of the major firms only Edmunds and Co of Church Street weathered the storm.

In Trowbridge, however, there were only two bankruptcies, both of men who used their premises for commission work, one dyeing and scouring and the other finishing. Clarks showed a profit in every year except 1842, when they lost ten per cent. In the 1830s they added to their Duke Street factory three times; one addition was to instal spinning mules, of which three pairs were bought in 1837. The first mules in the district were erected in 1828, probably at the Malmesbury factory of C.S. Taylor and Co, whose main site was at Chippenham; six mules were sold at Malmesbury when the firm was bankrupt in 1830.

Few mules were used in Yorkshire then; the west was not seriously behind in the adoption of machinery, and in certain fields led the way. Although the idea of shearing the cloth by using a rotating cutter (like a lawnmower, an appliance actually derived *from* the cloth industry) had been attempted before 1800, the main effort in perfecting these machines came from Gloucestershire and the United States. An early example may have been the 'perpetual shearing machine' for sale at Salisbury in 1807, but Clarks were probably typical of the more advanced clothiers, in changing from shearing-frames to cutters in the 1820s. The west led in fulling too. The rotary machine still used in the industry today resulted from the patent taken out by John Dyer of Trowbridge in 1833; he sold it to a Leeds man but reserved the right to make it himself. By 1847 a Leeds firm was advertising fulling machines in the west, saying that they were sole contractors, but lists of machinery show that Dyer also continued to make them. Dyer's invention did not cause the disappearance of fulling by stocks, which were preferred for some classes of work, and there was only a gradual erosion of the number of mills; Ladydown at Trowbridge and Welsh Mill at Frome survived into the present century.

Hadans of Trowbridge patented several improvements to existing machines, especially an arrangement by which the teazles in the gig were made to move from side to side as the drum rotated. The most prolific local patentee was Joseph Clisild Daniell, who lived at Limpley Stoke and was a partner in the mill at Twerton. His most far-reaching invention was that known as roll-boiling, which involved immersing the cloth in hot water, and gave it a damp-resistant finish.

Another report on the employment of children, made in 1833, tells of children who frequently started work at eight years old, and worked from 6 am to 8 pm, with two hours for meals, but the enquiry found that conditions in the west were generally good compared with elsewhere. The workpeople were well-dressed and respectable, and the children in general healthy. Mutual respect existed between employers and employed, and the clothiers were anxious for the welfare of their people. Corporal punishment of the children was seldom practised, and light where it did exist. Two Trowbridge clothiers were condemned for not stopping their engines at meal times and agreed to do so, and Dunkirk Factory was running a continuous 15 hours. The picture is perhaps a little too favourable, for the evidence came from the largest and best-run factories, but it is generally convincing.

Long and irregular hours were characteristic of water-powered mills. This could have its good side – the children at Spring Gardens near Frome would sing

> 'Slade's and Napper's are shut down
> There's no water up to town'

as they played while their own factory was stopped – but a later reminiscence shows that, after a weekend, Sheppard's Spring Gardens mill would sometimes work from midnight on Sunday to 10 am on Monday, and start again at 5 pm to take advantage of the full pond. In such circumstances the hands never took their clothes off during the week.

Another report to Parliament in 1840 shows that larger clothiers had not reduced piece rates, because their object was to get good work, but frequent under-employment effectively reduced wages actually earned. Older or poorer weavers took lower rates from smaller masters, with consequent likelihood of having truck payments imposed. Some favoured weavers, however, would be able to get more chains than they could weave, and would dispose of them to others at a lower rate, or employ other weavers to work at night, while they slept. It was thought that a third of the weavers were in good circumstances, a third as well-off as farm workers, and a third worse off. The weavers were indignant at the thought of being on a level with agricultural labourers. They also disliked working in factory conditions, though the practice of having some shop looms at the factories was becoming more common. The first power-looms in the area were set up at Staverton and at Heytesbury in 1839, but significant numbers did not appear until much later.

The North Bradley parish records bear out what was said about variations among the weavers. One pauper had a son who had work from Salters worth 14s a week and from Stancombs worth 7s, while another had two sons, both weavers, in full work earning 21s a week each, one of whom also rented land and milked six cows, while the other kept a chandler's shop. Their father lived with a son-in-law and had plenty of work quilling for his loom. Another claimant for relief worked for Webbs at Trowbridge, but only got a chain once in 12 weeks, which had to be woven by another man at a discount because the recipient was almost blind. Another claimant with a family was a good weaver, who only earned 5s 6d a week because of his dissolute and intemperate habits, according to the parish officers. Deeds of cottage property in the weaving villages such as Bradley, Southwick, and Dilton Marsh bear out the fact that there were properous weavers who could invest in houses and then make money by letting them.

Dyehouses at Court Street, Trowbridge, from a photograph of 1873. (WRO)

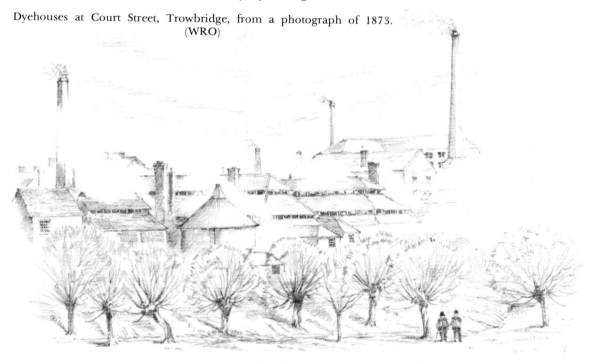

A *Return of Mills and Factories* made in 1838, provides this table:

	Woollen Mills	Silk Mills	Steam hp	No. of Engines	Water hp	No of Wheels
Wiltshire	48	4	706	40	336	40
Somerset	20	8	276	16	303	33

This must under-estimate the potential of the industry, by leaving out the water-powered fulling mills, of which at least a dozen were still working; the dyehouses, and especially factories at a standstill. Bradford, for instance, was said to have only four factories using five engines of 86 hp and eight wheels of 88 hp. It also had four large water-driven factories, and at least four steam-driven ones.

In Wiltshire significant factories remained at Trowbridge (19), Westbury (eight), Bradford (four), Bratton and Calne (three), Melksham (two), and Chippenham, Heytesbury, Holt and Malmesbury (one). Three little factories survived near Salisbury, one at Corsley, and one at Christian Malford. In Somerset the main centres were Frome (including Rodden) with five factories, Twerton and Freshford with two each, and Rode with one. Ten small mills were all on streams round Frome.

At the depth of the depression one of the Parliamentary commissions considered that 'the south of England clothiers must yield to the superior local advantages of the north'. They certainly suffered by comparison in the price paid for coal and the cost of transport of such as wool and oil. A smaller proportion of steam power was used than in Yorkshire, though Wiltshire was above the national average, largely owing to the emergence of Trowbridge as 'the Manchester of the west', a phrase employed from time to time by its fond inhabitants. Another charge levelled against the west in a Parliamentary paper was that the clothiers wasted capital by 'large establishments and expensive habits of living'. It is difficult to make a judgement. Large and elaborate houses *were* built, such as The Prospect in Trowbridge or Berryfield at Bradford both in the 1840s, but Samuel Salter, who died in 1851 worth £350,000, continued to live in the centre of Trowbridge. Successful clothiers had always invested in property, and income from it could act in two directions; it might diminish efforts to make a business prosperous, or it might enable bad times to be weathered.

Factories built at Cradle Bridge, Trowbridge, 1820s and 1830s, photographed 1873. (WRO)

ABOVE: Bitham Mill, Westbury, 1849. (WRO) BELOW: Cloth warehouses,
Stallard Street, Trowbridge.

ABOVE: Suppliers to factories. BELOW: Weaving shop with loom, probably Bradford, c1890. (BPT)

Weavers' houses: ABOVE: Trowbridge Road, Bradford; LEFT: Newtown, Trowbridge, and RIGHT: Thomas Street, Trowbridge.

Weaving shops: ABOVE LEFT: New Road, Trowbridge; RIGHT: Mortimer Street, Trowbridge, and CENTRE: Chapmanslade (now two cottages), dated 1821. BELOW: A Trowbridge heddle and slay maker, 1861. RIGHT: A weaving shop for sale, Warp Lane, Southwick, 1872.

Indian Summer

An upturn in trade began in 1843, and marked the beginning of a period of fairly sustained prosperity. It was checked briefly by the national depression of 1847–8, when the railway bubble burst. This brought down the largest Westbury firm, Matravers and Overbury, which had run three factories there, while at Trowbridge, Stancomb and Wilkins and at Frome, W. and J. Rossiter also stopped. After a few years the factories at Westbury were brought back into use. Abraham Laverton bought Angel Mill, which had been converted to grind corn, and re-started it in 1850, while Joseph and James Harrop moved to Wiltshire from the Saddleworth area of Yorkshire, and took a lease of Bitham Mill in 1851. John Rossiter, presumably from Frome, was at Boyers Mill, Westbury Leigh, but his machinery there was sold under a sheriff's order. He was succeeded by J. and J. Harrop, after they were bankrupt at Bitham Mill, which was then taken over by Abraham Laverton. Laverton, the son of a Trowbridge weaver, was a self-made man who built up a large fortune, and for a period ran four factories in Westbury. At an unknown date William Matravers re-started the Town Mill in Westbury, while Hawkeridge Mill just outside the town, which had stopped when Matravers and Overbury failed, was empty for a few years and then let to a firm from Trowbridge, J. Dicks and Son.

This picture of a reviving industry was repeated at Bradford, though two of its largest factories, Kingston Mill and Greenland Lower Mill, were converted for rubber manufacture. But the extensive Greenland Upper Mill, which appears to have been little used since 1841, was re-started by J.W. Applegate, who moved from Trowbridge, while another Trowbridge man, William Wilkins, moved to the steam-driven factory in Mason's Lane. Bullpit Factory started again in 1850, and Bridge Foot Mill in 1867. Outside the town, Limpley Stoke Mill was working by 1852, though its history as a cloth mill ended a year later, when it was gutted by fire.

In those years the Frome trade was dominated by the old-established firm of Sheppards, who had three adjoining factories at Spring Gardens and another at Rodden, as well as a dyehouse in Willow Vale. Three other firms of size were running – Houston and Son of Vallis Way and Broadway, Harry Hams of the Butts, South Parade, and Egford, and Magill and Stephens of Wallbridge.

On the River Frome above the town two small water-driven factories still survived, while below it were factories at Staplemead (to which Sinkins and Wood moved from Hapsford in Great Elm in 1859), Scutts Bridge at Rode, Farleigh Hungerford and Freshford, the latter re-started after being empty for some years. There was a large custom dyehouse at Shawford near Beckington.

The outpost of the industry at Twerton had once had three separate factory sites, but after c1830 only one firm remained. Charles Wilkins and Co was said to be the largest in the area in 1833, employing 800 hands in two factories and 200–300 outside; it was succeeded at Twerton by Isaac Carr and Co, though they only kept one of the factories. North of Chippenham nothing remained, for the factory at Malmesbury turned to silk after 1852, and the two at Christian Malford and Avon stopped about then and were pulled down. At Chippenham only Rawlings and Pocock at Waterford Mill remained. The largest factory at Calne, Horsebrook Mill, was given up by Joseph Bailey and Co, and subsequently became a flax mill, but for a short time the trade was revived, probably at Hole Mill, by Dowding and Co, who were primarily paper makers. At Melksham the one factory was taken over in 1862 by Matravers and Son, whose Town Mill at Westbury had been destroyed by fire. Holt still had one factory, while Staverton, empty since 1841, was re-started in 1866. At Bratton the largest of the three factories was empty for some years after the bankruptcy of England and Son in 1855, but was used in the 1870s by a firm of scribblers from Trowbridge. Above it two small scribbling mills remained in use, while south of Warminster was the large factory at Upton Lovell.

Trowbridge continued to hold the premier position assumed with the coming of steam; over a dozen large factories and four dyehouses were in use in the late 1850s. It also became a considerable centre for the sale of cloth, for many firms sent less and less to London, sometimes selling direct by sending travellers out. Several prosperous firms of merchants came into being after 1850, selling locally-made cloth and goods bought from the north. Wool merchants were also based in the town; one firm dealt in waste and re-converted it to yarn, occupying first a factory at Bradford, then one at Bratton, and finally building one in the Conigre. Another way of using the waste dust from carding was to make it into felt hats, a trade carried on at Trowbridge and Frome, while flock for bedding was made at Avoncliff, Freshford, and elsewhere.

Trowbridge, and to some extent Frome as well, were the last refuge of the small clothier without a factory, of whom some remained in business into the 1870s. Some still had workshops. Samuel Morris of Union Street, Trowbridge in 1840 had two scribbling and one carding engines and a billy, and was still in business in 1867. William Tanner of Frog Lane had three jennies in 1855, and Jacob Cogswell was using spinning shops in Newtown in 1863. Such men would have had work done on commission, rented individual machines in factories, and put work out to weavers. Working in this way, William Collier made at least 175 cloths in the years 1846–1849, and also dealt in teazles, oil, soap, and cloth. He often paid his debts in these articles. A clothier on the smallest scale was Abraham Gayton of Hilperton who, in 1851, employed his wife as a clothworker, a daughter as a burler, and three sons as weavers and spinners. A proposal in 1871 to establish a joint stock to work a mill in Trowbridge was presumably aimed at the small clothiers, but came to nothing.

A flourishing trade promoted prosperity in many other fields. Steam engines could be bought locally from Hadens of Trowbridge, Fisher and Rodgers both of Frome, or Spencer and Gillett of Melksham, while local machinery makers were Millard and Sons of Ashton Iron Works, Trowbridge, and Abraham Haley of Selwood Iron Works, Frome, both of whom specialised in looms. Shuttles were made at Trowbridge and Melksham, and harnesses and slays for hand looms were still made in the area. Frome remained a centre for making card clothing, and the firms of Samuel Rawlings and Son in South Parade and George Hinchcliffe at Portway were nationally known. A Bradford cardmaking firm was bankrupt in 1870. At Frome also, James Holroyd was a dyestuff manufacturer, and logwood mills were at Twerton and Keynsham.

Supplying the factories with coal must have been an industry in itself. Samuel Brown's factory at Trowbridge, with a 20 hp engine, used 337 tons of engine coal in three months in 1853, all of which was brought by boat to Hilperton Marsh and then hauled into the town.

Piecing machines, which replaced the billy, to join together the lengths of carded wool, were brought in by some firms in the 1850s, but became obsolete on the introduction of a method of 'condensing'. This enabled the carding engine to produce continuous slubbings, which were wound off on to reels ready to go in the mules. This important invention had reached our area by the late 1850s. By that time the jenny had disappeared from all but the smallest factories in favour of the mule; Clarks of Trowbridge had eight in 1843, though they were then still using jennies, to some of which power had been applied. These early mules were not self-acting but, like the jenny, relied on the skill of the spinner to produce even yarn. It is not known when the self-actor first appeared in the west.

Clarks were using all rotary cutters in 1843, and certainly by that time the shearing frame was obsolete. By this time, too, washers for cloth were generally used, replacing the former method of braying by using stocks. Wool washing machines came after 1850, but much wool was still scoured in the old way in the 1870s, when Trowbridge manufacturers had to take their wool to Shawford because of the dirty state of the Biss.

Abbey Mill, Bradford.

It was only in the 1840s that the powerloom was sufficiently perfect to weave fine cloth, and its general introduction into factories came in the next decade. Clarks of Trowbridge built a powerloom shed in 1858 and extended it in 1865, while Brown and Palmer built a new one in 1860. At Broughton Gifford in 1859 the powerloom had displaced hand weaving for all broad goods, and only fancy goods woven narrow were still done in the cottages. Cloth with an elaborate pattern needed a loom with a Jacquard mechanism, and this was used at Staverton before 1870. When Webb's factory at Trowbridge was sold up in 1896 it was almost entirely fitted with narrow looms (made by Haley of Frome), with Jacquard mechanisms. The weaving shed there was dated 1868, so presumably the powerloom was taking over the fancy trade as well about then. But the woollen industry never cared much for the Jacquard mechanism, and semi-fancy looms of the Dobcross or Hattersley varieties were much more common in local sheds.

In 1859 at Broughton Gifford hand weavers were hard at work 14 hours a day to turn out four to six yards, at 10d, 8d or 6d a yard. Each weaver had to have a child, or perhaps two, to change his shuttles (this would have been for fancy work), and one to wind the quills. By then to get a chain was a matter for satisfaction, and there was often little or no work. In earlier times a weaver had often kept a pony to take in his cloth and bring his yarn back. Now he was lucky if he had a pair of trucks – if not he had to walk with his work in a white bag slung over his shoulder, subjected to the teasing of children, who knew that if he put it down he would need help to pick it up again.

Weaving shops were usually in the principal downstairs room of a house rather than in a separate building or lean-to. The only exceptions were the terraces of three-storeyed houses common in Trowbridge, where the top-floor was the shop. These were mainly built between 1790 and 1830, when cassimeres were the town's main product. Several noted weaving villages are said to have worked largely for particular firms – Salters of Trowbridge had theirs done at Bromham, while Clarks sent narrow cloth to Dilton Marsh and broad to Bradford. Two handlooms which survived into the present century at Palmer and McKay's factory at Trowbridge differed in their degree of sophistication; one, thought to be 18th century, needed 16 pedals to work ten harnesses, while an early 19th–century loom had a simple dobby mechanism, which meant that two treadles would work ten harnesses, and also had a fly-shuttle.

The last handloom weavers worked into the 1870s, partly owing to the pretence which they fostered and the clothiers (erroneously) believed, that certain types of cloth, such as whipcords, were better woven on handlooms. A woman weaver at Palmer and MacKays at Trowbridge, bringing a breach of promise action against the man who gave the work out in 1878, said that he stopped giving her chains when they fell out, but he said that trade was so bad that it had been given up as far as possible. Moore and Edmonds of Freshford appear to have used all hand weavers until they were bankrupt in 1878. Some other processes could be done domestically; three references to jennies in houses, all from Trowbridge, have been found between 1841 to 1862, and doubling by machine was done at home there as late as 1868.

In 1863 the powerloom weavers at Joseph Harrop's Boyers Mill at Westbury Leigh struck, because they had been fined on the evidence of an 11–year old time-keeper who had no clock. They were supported by donations from Trowbridge, and a United Weavers' Association was formed. It was said two years later that its object was to arrange things with the masters and prevent strikes, and that several such arrangements had been successfully made. No more is known of it, but there was little industrial trouble. The papers, reporting treats given to workpeople and retirements of old hands, regularly spoke of good feeling between masters and their workpeople, and it seems to have been widespread and genuine.

By the later 1850s, the prosperity of the last few years had been sustained for long enough to induce clothiers to invest, not only in new machinery, but in building. Weaving sheds were added to most factories where land was available; Clarks of Trowbridge had no space at Duke Street, so in 1857 they bought a smaller factory near the Town Bridge, and replaced it by the present Studley Mill, a complete factory with a four-storeyed carding and spinning block as well as weaving sheds. Brown and Palmer added a complete new factory, Ashton Mill, to their Courts Mill in 1860. At Frome the Vallis Way factory of Henry Houston and Son was also largely rebuilt by 1866, while Wallbridge Mill appears to date from the years immediately after 1868, when it had passed into the ownership of a Trowbridge cloth merchant, W.H. Tucker, who set up his son in trade. At Trowbridge two factories were also rebuilt after fire: Home Mills of Samuel Salter and Co in 1862 and Innox Mill of James Cogswell in 1875.

The new factories were no longer the tall narrow buildings of earlier times. The blocks were square in plan so that they could accommodate the mules and carding sets. Perhaps the handsomest example is Abbey Mill at Bradford, built by Harper, Taylor and Little in 1875 to replace the older seven-storey factory. Its designer was Richard Gane the younger, a Trowbridge-born architect in practice in London.

In 1866 a Trowbridge butcher held a public meeting at Pewsey, well to the east of Devizes, to propose raising capital to set up a cloth factory there. It was thought that £10,000 would be required for buildings, £20,000 for machinery, and £15,000 for working capital. The idea came to nothing, but it is indicative of the mood of optimism.

Innovation had also extended to the types of cloth made. By 1840 fancy stripes and tweeds were being made at Trowbridge, and an advertisment to let Bulkington Mill in 1848 said that it was well-placed for the fancy goods trade so extensively carried on at Trowbridge. Other special lines were developed from traditional types of cloth. Sheppards of Frome claimed to have introduced Venetians, a black broadcloth woven with a twill, but it became a speciality in Bradford, Staverton, Melksham, Chippenham, and Upton Lovell. The finest of all were said to have been made at Holt. Upton Lovell and Twerton were noted for beavers, a heavily-milled cloth with a raised finish resulting in a nap like a beaver's fur. Other cloths which relied on a special finish were doeskins and moleskins, both of which were exhibited by Trowbridge firms at the Great Exhibition in 1851, where Clarks, Stancombs, and Salters all won medals, as did Carrs of Twerton. But smaller firms built up good reputations for particular cloths too; the finest doeskins in the world were, it was claimed, produced by Charles Salter and Co of Farleigh Hungerford.

An account of Frome firms in 1866 shows how they specialised in different lines: Sheppards made doeskins, Venetians and every description of fancy goods, Houstons treble and double milled doeskins and Bedford and drab cords, and Magill and Stephens Meltons, cloths with a special soft finish, in contrast to the rather hard glazed look which had been popular a few years earlier. Sinkins and Wood were more in the traditional way of Frome trade, making broadcloths of various colours used for liveries, and it was said that they had to be careful in preserving the exact colours traditional in various noble families. Harry Hams also made liveries as well as cords and tweeds.

Another exhibition was held in 1862, and the report on textiles referred to important improvements in technique since 1851. These included machines for scouring and drying wool, the condenser and the patent feed invented by James Apperley of Gloucestershire to make the scribbling and carding processes continuous, the self-acting mule, improvements to powerlooms to make them suited for fancy work, and tentering machines to do away with the necessity of outdoor drying. Some artificial dyes were coming into use, and the quality of the Australian wool now in common use was having an important effect on finish. The report went on to say that Trowbridge and Westbury had fully kept pace with the times, and showed considerable progress in manufacturing power, increase of trade, and economy of production since 1851. Four local firms, Carrs of Twerton, Edmunds of Bradford, Lavertons of Westbury, and Salters of Trowbridge won medals in the fine cloth section, while Hewitts of Heytesbury, Stancomb Brothers of Trowbridge, and Sheppards of Frome were honourably mentioned.

That the West of England remained unrivalled for quality cloth is clear from the general comments on this and later exhibitions. That it was not behind in technical matters is vouched for by an article on the Paris exhibition of 1867 in a Yorkshire newpaper. Asking a series of rhetorical questions, the writer compared his own area with the west: 'Who first turned their attention to more careful wool scouring and washing? Who retained truth in their carding engines by not unduly extending their width to obtain quantity at expence of quality? Who have adopted improved fixing for these machines while our overlookers have been tapping or rapping their worker shaft ends to make them bed in their clumsy, loose, ill-fitting bearings? Who further adopted the condenser when the blood of our pieceners was lubricating the clumsy overlap joints of the cardings in our antiquated sloobing process? Who were spinning away upon Platt's self-acting mules ten years or more ago while we were hesitating and ordering hand mules? Who invented and adopted the milling machine?'

Weaving sheds added to factories: ABOVE: Greenland Mill, Bradford (BPT)
and BELOW: Studley Mill, Trowbridge.

Factories of the later period: ABOVE: Ashton Mill, Trowbridge, to right, with earlier Courts Mill to left, photographed 1873; LEFT: Home Mill, Trowbridge, also 1873, (Both WRO) and RIGHT: Wallbridge Mill, Frome (FM)

ABOVE: Clarks of Trowbridge entertain their workpeople at Wingfield, c1880. (WRO) BELOW: The rewards of success: Belcombe Court, Bradford, home of the Yerbury family. (BPT)

LEFT: Samuel Salter of Trowbridge, who died worth £350,000 in 1850. (TM)
RIGHT: Frome Literary and Scientific Institute, given by John Sinkins of
Staplemead Mill, 1868. BELOW: John Bayfield Clark of Trowbridge and his
family at Wingfield, c1870. (WRO)

ABOVE: Trowbridge Cottage Hospital, given in memory of Jesse
Gouldsmith, 1833. BELOW: Roger Brown of Trowbridge, third from right,
shooting on his estate at Brokerswood, c1890. (WRO)

The Final Curtain

In 1876 the *Trowbridge Advertiser,* commenting on the present extraordinary depression, wrote 'Trowbridge and its sister manufacturing towns have kept pace with every improvement. . .but in the last year or two the demand for this class of high-priced cloth seems to be declining. . .the less durable, more fanciful and lower-priced class of cloth introduced by the Scotch manufacturers is superseding the West of England. . .Where one piece of West of England is sold now 100 pieces of the lower-priced fancy Scotch are readily purchased.' The writer went on to put the opposing viewpoints of the firms: on one side that the change was likely to be permanent, on the other that, if the old-established staple trade was given up, it could never return.

Yet another exhibition, at Paris in 1878, prompted an article in the *Leeds Mercury,* which was again complimentary about the quality of western cloth. 'The fancy trouserings and silk mixtures of Salter and Co. are all that could be desired in quality and perfection', said the writer; 'No country could show better-made goods than the fine beavers and meltons of Isaac Carr and Co. of Bath'. But he went on, 'The productions of the West of England rank second to none in the world, though few but Englishmen can afford to wear them. French and German goods may be preferred for price but not for quality. When the fine cloth trade of America was transferred from the West of England to Germany it was a matter more of price than of quality and make.'

In the late 1870s, however, the spectre which haunted the west came from Scotland. The makers of fancy tweeds from the borders offered a particular threat to the fancy goods trade of Trowbridge. A correspondent of the local paper in 1876 contrasted the prosperity of Scotland with the worst situation in Trowbridge for 20 years, and blamed the rise of the ready-made clothes factories, and the widespread use of the sewing machine in families, for the fact that people wanted lower-priced cloths. Other letters followed, some saying that the west should not panic, that the vogue for Scottish cloth was temporary, and trade would revive, others that the Scottish styles must be imitated. In 1877 a Trowbridge firm advertised for a designer and pattern weaver able to imitate fancy twilled coatings and trouserings and cheviots, and another firm also advertised for a designer of tweeds. Yorkshire too had learnt from Scotland, and was now producing fancy coatings made from a mixture of woollen and worsted yarn. It was no doubt this that prompted Lavertons of Westbury to begin using some worsted yarn as early as 1875.

It was probably this competition which again started the closure of factories, largely ceased since 1855. Of just under 50 factories active in that year (to which three new ones were subsequently added), only three stopped in the 1860s, two because they were burnt down and not rebuilt – Town Mill at Westbury and Masons Lane factory at Bradford – and one, Wellhead at Westbury, in unknown circumstances. The later 1870s saw several firms go out of business. J. Dicks and Sons of Hawkeridge near Westbury, and Moore and Edmunds at Freshford were both bankrupt, and neither factory was used in the industry again. These were not large businesses, but Sheppards at Frome, which closed in 1878, ran one of the largest concerns, making 5,000 yards a week a few years earlier. They had three large factory buildings at Spring Gardens and a dyehouse in the centre of Frome. The former Sheppard factory at Rodden, under its then style of Frome Woollen Mills, also shut about this time, and none of these Frome buildings were used again.

Sheppards were not insolvent, but presumably did not consider it worthwhile to continue and make only small profits. The family was wealthy, and could bear the loss which must have been incurred in selling the machinery and buildings. The buildings at Spring Gardens only made £720.

Only for Clarks of Trowbridge is a long series of profit figures available, and it is notable that their best profits came just after the period of severe depression; they made over 15 per cent in 1844 and almost 12 per cent in 1845. They never exceeded 8 per cent in the 40 years following, and were much more commonly below 4 per cent, but they only made a loss on one year, in 1858. 1874 onwards was certainly bad for them: in that year and 1875 they made under 1 per cent, and did not exceed 3 per cent until 1883. J.H. Webb and Sons of Bridge Mill had a partnership between two of the sons of J.H. Webb and Edward Dyer, which allowed the three working partners to take stated salaries and then divide the profits; from 1874 to 1883 (when information ceases) they only reached the total needed to pay the salaries once, and then only just.

Profit figures for firms in the Bradford–Trowbridge–Westbury area are also available from a series of income-tax returns covering most years between 1873 and 1885, and they too suggest that most firms were making enough to provide a modest living for the partners in what were still family businesses. Progressive firms might have been doing better, for Salters and Brown and Palmer, both of Trowbridge, appear to have been little affected by the bad years after 1874. It is remarkable, nevertheless, that the Bradford firm of Harper, Taylor, and Little should have built Abbey Mill, an elaborate new factory, in 1875. In about the same year Clarks of Trowbridge added a second carding and spinning building to their Studley Mill, and their neighbours Webbs built new mule shops on to their factory in 1877. Just across the road the Innox Mill of James Cogswell, burnt in 1875, was immediately rebuilt, and let to Hewitt and Kemp, who removed Hewitt's trade from Upton Lovell.

Perhaps progressive firms were trying to combat bad times by increasing efficiency by further investment. One Trowbridge firm, J. and E. Hayward of Upper Mill, was thought to have become bankrupt in 1878 because they had overstretched themselves in new buildings and machinery, and the factory was certainly well-equipped. There were two other bankruptcies at Trowbridge in the 1870s. James Adye of Victoria Mill was a comparatively new firm, and attempted to rescue his ailing business by over-insuring his old-fashioned factory and machinery and then setting it on fire. The other firm which failed was that of J.W. Gabriel of Yerbury Street, whose business career of 30 years ended in 1876 in circumstances verging on fraud. In Westbury J. and J. Harrop of Boyers Mill stopped in 1874 on the death of Joseph Harrop. An attempt was made to form a company to carry on the trade, by raising £15,000, of which about £4,000 would be required to buy the machinery at a valuation. Two years earlier Harrop had said that he had invested £7,000 in plant, a clear indication of the losses the firms had to take if they closed their mills.

In fact Boyers was taken over by Abraham Laverton, whose business had in the course of 20 years become one of the biggest in the area. His success at making money was only partly owing to his trade, for his fortune came largely from speculation in the money market. Laverton sat as a Liberal MP for the Westbury borough seat, and his benefactions to the town were numerous. Another man in the same mould was Roger Brown of Trowbridge, who built up the small business he took over in 1853 into the largest concern in Trowbridge; he too made money from speculation and from a considerable investment in property. A third self-made man was a younger contemporary of these, William Walker, who started as a traveller for his father, one of the smallest manufacturers in Trowbridge. Prospering in this, Walker and his brother bought Stone Mill (which J. and T. Clark had rented from 1849 to 1870) and began making cloth. Walker was able to buy the Yerbury Street Mill vacated by Gabriel in 1877, and then the business and two factories of Samuel Salter and Co in 1885. A year later he bought the factory at Upton Lovell, and until after the turn of the century was running five factories together.

Another Trowbridge factory, that of Haywards, quickly found other occupants in the firm of Edward Kemp, subsequently Kemp and Stevens, who also ran the large custom dyehouse on the River Frome at Shawford near Beckington. It was not until 1883 that a Trowbridge factory passed out of the industry; this was the Duke Street Mill of J. and T. Clark, converted to a flour mill when they concentrated on the Studley Mill site. In 1888 the small firm of Benjamin Perkins and Co closed their Court Street factory. Elsewhere the factory at Holt stopped in 1885, and was pulled down, and the last one at Melksham was sold up in 1888. At Bradford the small Bullpit Factory was destroyed by fire.

Scutts Bridge Mill, Rode, pulled down when in ruins a few years ago.

The contraction was probably due to comparatively expensive cloth in a restricted market. The machinery in the up-to-date mills was so much larger and faster that production was probably greater than it had been 50 years earlier, but the market had not expanded to keep pace. Many of those who could afford to wear West of England cloth lived in the United States, and it was disastrous that entry tariffs rose in 1883 and again in 1890, for the rises encouraged the manufacture of fine cloth there. Clark's had a good spell of profits in the later 1880s, but from 1891 they slumped progressively to an actual loss in 1896, the last year for which figures are known.

Closures continued in the 1890s and early into the present century. At Trowbridge, Webbs closed in 1896 and Stancombs in 1905. Ward and Taylor closed their two Bradford factories in 1898, and an attempt from outside the area to re-start them proved abortive. Hargreaves and Co of Staverton ended their run-down concern in 1891, and an attempt to re-use the factory to manufacture cloth from wool scoured by a new patent process ended in fiasco. The end of the industry in Bradford came with the closure of Applegates at Greenland Upper Mill in 1905. H.J. Rawlings and Co of Frome, who had factories in the town and at Staplemead, stopped in 1904. Scutts Bridge Mill at Rode closed at the same time, the last water-driven factory, and the last country mill, at Farleigh Hungerford, was sold up in 1910, Upton Lovell having been burnt down in 1898.

At this point contraction largely ceased, though the one factory at Chippenham was badly damaged by fire in 1915 and was only a small business when it finally closed in 1930. The remainder, consisting of five firms at Trowbridge, two at Frome, and one each at Westbury and Twerton, survived until after the Second World War. The final period of closures began with Houstons of Frome in 1945, and ended when Salters of Trowbridge, by then only a weaving outpost of the Illingworth-Morris combine, was closed in 1982. The magic of the West of England name did not prove sufficient in the end to enable firms to cope with fierce competition from other fabrics, and when exporters were at the mercy of adverse international trading conditions.

The main part of the old manufacturing area, in west Wiltshire and the Frome area, remains a busy industrial district, with many businesses which started in and often still use, the former factories. Although there have been sad demolitions, a number of impressive buildings still remain, and it is much to be hoped that the best of them can be successfully converted to modern use as offices, workshops or homes, to preserve a visual memory of such an ancient and notable industy.

Spring Gardens Mill, Frome, in decay c1880.

HAWKERIDGE,

One Mile from the Town of Westbury and Three from Trowbridge.

Sale of a Freehold Woollen MILL, with valuable Water Power, Capital Steam Engine and Boiler, and a Piece of Excellent Pasture Land, with Cottage and Garden.

MR. J. G. FOLEY,

IS FAVOURED WITH INSTRUCTIONS TO

SELL BY AUCTION,
At the Commercial Sale Room, Trowbridge,

ON TUESDAY, MARCH the 15th, 1864,

At SIX o'Clock in the Evening (subject to such Conditions as will be then produced) ALL THAT VALUABLE

WOOLLEN MILL,

Situated at Hawkeridge in the Parish of Westbury, in the County of Wilts, together with the Capital Piece of WATER MEADOW and GARDEN LAND thereto adjoining comprising 4½ Acres or thereabouts.

THE MILL is substantially brick-built and tiled, with good Roof and Main Timbers, is 64 feet long by 22 feet 10 inches wide, having 4 Floors and a top Store Loft, with Foreman's House; together with a NEW NORTH WING of 2 Floors, each 54 feet long by 20 feet 6 inches wide, with a new Tucking Shop, Engine House, &c., ALSO THE CAPITAL

8-HORSE POWER
STEAM ENGINE & BOILER,
(By Fisher of Frome.)

An Excellent Water Wheel and the whole of the running Gear Work, Shafting and Fixtures throughout the Mill.

N.B. There is an excellent supply of Water with a capital Iron Frame and Apparatus for shutting off the water from the Mill during repairs.

LOT 2—ALL THAT COTTAGE with the piece of GARDEN LAND thereto adjoining and belonging, situated at North Leaze at Hawkeridge aforesaid, and near to the Mill, and containing about half an Acre.

For Leave to View apply on the Premises, and for Further Particulars to the AUCTIONEER, the Parade, Trowbridge, or to

ROWLAND RODWAY, ESQ.,
SOLICITOR, TROWBRIDGE.

PRINTED BY MACHINERY, (AT THE ADVERTISER OFFICE), BY B. LANSDOWN, TROWBRIDGE.

Hawkeridge Mill, Westbury for sale, 1864.

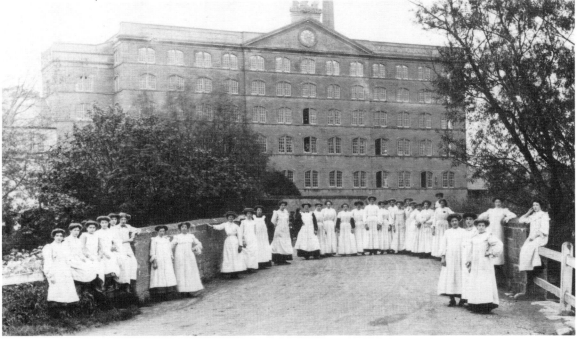

ABOVE: Avoncliff, former a fulling mill, converted for making flock, c1880.
BELOW: Staverton Factory, in use as a milk condensery, c1905.

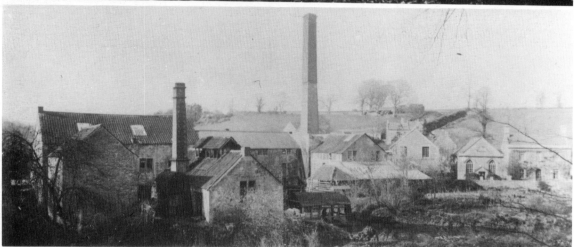

ABOVE: Scutts Bridge Mill, Rode, the last water-driven mill, closed c1904.
CENTRE: Farleigh Hungerford Mill, the last country factory, closed
1910.(DP) LEFT: Waterford Mill, Chippenham, gutted by fire, 1915. (CM)
RIGHT: Home Mill, Trowbridge, gutted by fire, 1931.

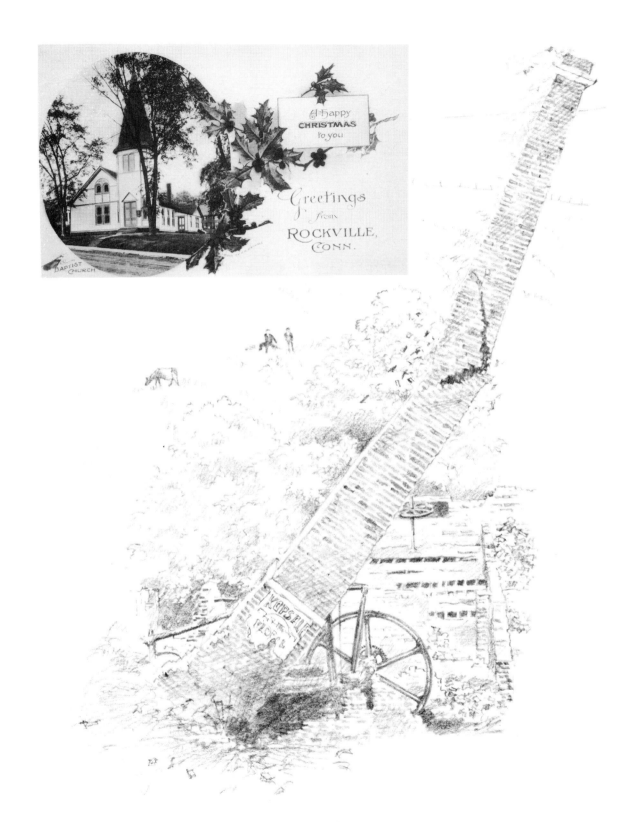

A Happy CHRISTMAS to you

Greetings from ROCKVILLE, CONN.

BAPTIST CHURCH

Bratton, Stradbrook Mill: felling of chimney and destruction of Boulton and Watt engine. INSET: At the last, many clothworkers emigrated, especially to Rockville, Connecticut, and Providence, Rhode Island.

Warp and Weft

While the processes changed as the industry grew, the essence of the conversion of raw wool to finished cloth remained – a complex set of skills involving an interlocking series of actions. In these final pictures, the entire business from wool to finished product is defined – through the people who made it happen, by the sweat of their collective brow, the dexterity of their many hands and the application of their total experience and judgement.

What started as a Saxon necessity, and ended as a modern casualty of mass-production, at its zenith was one of the finest manufactures of Britain when it was truly great. West of England cloth – the very words conjure up an image of superior finish, svelte appearance, quiet sophistication and sheer style. Whatever the trials of the workers, the oppression of the young, the chicaneries of clothiers, this product range was among the finest produced in England.

In these following pictures is truly represented the nature and the character of an industry – its warp and its weft.

Sorting wool, 1913.

ABOVE: Dyeing wool and cloth, 1930 and BELOW: carding, feed end, 1930.

ABOVE: Carding, condensing end, 1913. BELOW: Mule spinning,
1913.(FM)

Doubling, 1903.

ABOVE: Warping, 1913. BELOW: Drawing and tying on, *ie* making the warp threads pass through the heddles in the harnesses, 1913.

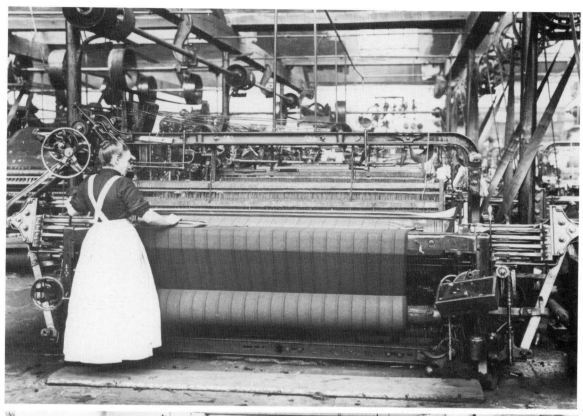

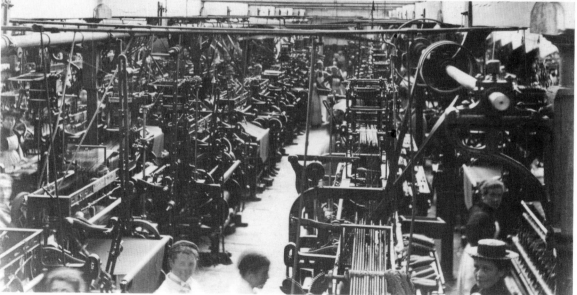

ABOVE: Weaving, 1903, and BELOW: on narrow looms made by Millards of Trowbridge, probably in a Bradford factory c1890. Some of the looms have Jacquard mechanisms. (BPT)

ABOVE: Quill winding, 1913. BELOW: Washing cloth, 1913.

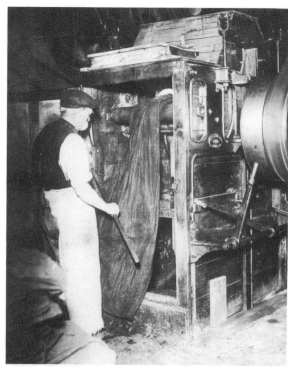

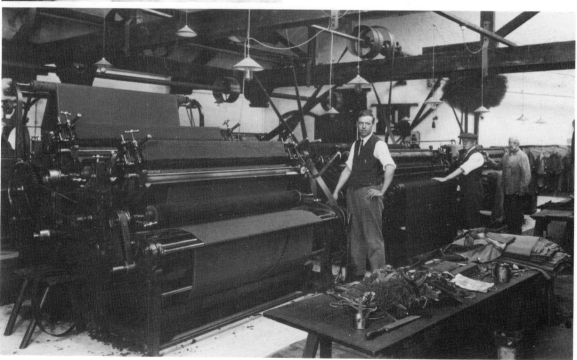

LEFT: Fulling, Dyer's patent machine, 1913; the man is measuring the shrinkage of the cloth. RIGHT: Cutting, 1913. Note the spiral blade right at the top of the machine. BELOW: Cutting, 1930.

ABOVE: Burling, 1913. BELOW: Bringing in a boiler, Salters, Trowbridge, c1920.

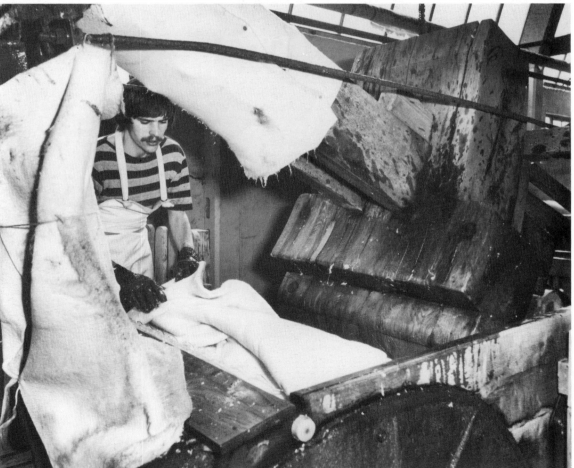

ABOVE: Weavers at Waterford Mill, Chippenham c1905. (CM) BELOW:
Fulling stocks still in use at E.V. Naish and Co's felt factory at Wilton,
1986.

The end product.

Bibliography

The starting point for all work on the West of England woollen industry is Julia de Lacy Mann's *The Cloth Industry in the West of England from 1640 to 1880* (Oxford 1971); attractively written and the product of deep research, its footnotes and bibliography form a detailed guide to sources for its subject. Miss Mann also wrote the later of two chapters on the industry in *Wiltshire Victoria County History* vol iv, while the earlier period was dealt with in brilliant fashion by Professor Eleonora Carus-Wilson. The chapter in *Somerset Victoria County History* vol ii, was written before the First World War, and is only useful as a repository of facts.

K.G. Ponting's two books, *A History of the West of England Cloth Industry* (Macdonald 1957) and *The Woollen Industry of South-West England* (Adams and Dart, 1971) both have much of value, especially where they reflect the author's practical experience as a manufacturer. Ken Ponting also co-operated with D.T. Jenkins in an excellent general history, *The British Wool Textile Industry 1770–1914* (Pasold Research Fund, 1982). G.D. Ramsay's *The Wiltshire Woollen Industry in the sixteenth and seventeenth centuries* (2nd edition, Oxford, 1965) is a gracefully-written study which has stood the test of time well. Some of the conclusions of A.R. Bridbury's *Medieval English Clothmaking: an Economic Survey* (Pasold, 1982) have been questioned by reviewers.

K.H. Rogers, *Wiltshire and Somerset Woollen Mills* (Pasold, 1976) contains a general study of the various types of industrial buildings followed by a gazetteer of sites. Other printed work of particular relevance is listed below.

The primary sources for the subject of this book are mainly in the Wiltshire Record Office in deposits made by the recently surviving firms – J. and T. Clark (WRO 927), Samuel Salter and Co (WRO 926), and Abraham Laverton and Co (WRO 954). Individual records of value include books of the Wansey family (WRO 314), Stephen Hillman (WRO 1090), Jeremiah Awdry (WRO 873), William Hussey (WRO 776). Files of the Salisbury and Trowbridge newspapers are also in the Wiltshire Record Office. At the Somerset Record Office is the letter book of James Elderton (DD/X/MSL).

Beckinsale, R.P. *The Trowbridge Woollen Industry, 1804–1824* (Wilts Record Soc vi).

Hall, A.R. and Russell, N.C., 'What about the Fulling-Mill? *History of Technology*, vi.

Leech, Roger, *Early Industrial Housing, The Trinity area of Frome* (HMSO, 1981)

Mann, J. de L. 'A Wiltshire Family of Clothiers; George and Hester Wansey' *Economic History Review*, 2nd series, ix, 2

'Clothiers and Weavers in Wiltshire in the eighteenth century', *Studies in the Industrial Revolution presented to T.S. Ashton*, ed L.S. Presnell (London 1960).

Partridge, William, *A Practical Treatise on Dying* (1823, reprinted Pasold 1973)

Rogers, K.H. 'Trowbridge Clothiers and their Houses', *Textile History and Economic History, Essays in Honour of Miss Julia de Lacy Mann* (Manchester 1973)

Tann, Jennifer, 'Power in the West-of-England Wool Industry' in *ibid*.

Index

Figures in *italics* refer to illustrations

Abbey Mill *85,111*
Adlam, William 20,40
Adye, James 120
Allen, Hall and Co. 69
Alleyne family 26
Andrews, Thomas . . 64,65
Anstie, John 68,73,
76,100
Apperley, James 113
Applegate family 109,
122
apprenticeship . . . 26,40,41
Ashe family 23,32
Ashton Mill *115*
Ashton, Steeple,
Wiltshire 22,24,26,
30,32
Avon Mill,
Malmesbury *89*
Avon, river *93*
Avoncliff near Bradford,
Wiltshire . . . 28,47,50,74,
76,84,*124*
Awdry family 34,43
Jeremiah, account
of *61*
Bailey family 24,25,26,
28,110
Bamford, Samuel
Paul 74,77
Barford St. Martin,
Wiltshire 80,81
Bartlee, James, workshop
of *43*
Baskervill, family 40
Batcombe, Somerset . . . 23,
32
Bath, Avon . . . 18,20,21,23,
24,35,39,68,101
Batheaston 100
Beaven, Thomas 40
Beckington, Somerset . . 21,
25,32,40,41,50,52,55,75,
76,77
Bedwyn, Wiltshire 14
Belcombe Court *116*
Bennett family 26
Billingsley and Bowles . . 47
Bisse, James 23
Bitham Mill *94,105*
Blackbarrow, Peter 26
Blackwell Hall,
London 18,25,26,28,
40,47,53,55,64
Blagden House 21
Blagden, William 28
boiler 1920 . . . . *136*
Boulton and Watt . . . 68,76,
77,81,82,*94,98,127*
Bourne, Daniel 67
Bowlish, Somerset . . . 44,48
Boyers Mill *75*
Boyton, Wiltshire 21
Bradford, Wiltshire 17
passim *37,38,41,79,101*

Bradley, North,
Wiltshire 26,74,103
Bratton, Wiltshire . . . 18,32,
53,*77*,80,82,84,
104,110,*127*
Brewer family 32,33,
34,41
Bridbury, Dr A.R. 16
Bridge Factory *96*
House,
Trowbridge *57*
Bridge Mill *95*
Bristol, Avon 18,23,25,
26,28,47,48,55,68,69,76
Brittain, Richard 99
Bromham, Wiltshire . . . 34,
112
Brooks, Richard 50,*59*
Brooks and Randall 48
Broughton Gifford,
Wiltshire 21,26,111
Brown, Roger *117*,121
Brown and Palmer . . . 111,
112,120
Bruton, Somerset . . . 21,23,
28,53,100
Bulford, Wiltshire 48
Bull Mill, Crockerton . . . *90*
Burley family 26
Bush, John 84
Bush, Newton and
Bush 76
Butcher, William 23
Calne, Wiltshire 26,33,
40,63,73,75,81,82,84,*86*,
100,101,104,110
Calstone, Wiltshire 26,
50,84,100
Cam family 41
canals 81
cardmaking 14,34
Carr, Isaac and Co 109,
113,119
Carus-Wilson,
Professor E 15
Castle Combe,
Wiltshire 18,21,23,
26,40
Market Cross *22*
Chard, Somerset 67,74
Chaunceler,
Thomas 20,21
Chew Magna, Avon 23,
36,39,40
Chilton Foliat,
Wiltshire 17
Chippenham,
Wiltshire . . 34,39,40,41,
42,68,69,73,75,76,78,80,
83,84,100,104,113
Chittoe, Wiltshire 63

Chiver family 28
Chistian Malford . . . 83,84,
104,109
Cirencester,
Gloucestershire 26
circular,1798 . . . . *92*
Clark family 41,43,*46*,
47,63,73,74,80,82,*98*,99,
100,110,111,112,113,
116,117,120
John Bayfield *117*

Clavey family 47
Clevelode, John 25
Clifford in Beckington,
Somerset 28,50
cloth, finishing *59*
cloth, varieties of:
beavers 54,113
burels 14
cassimeres 39,43,
50,65,68,74,76,80,83,
100,112
Castlecombes 18
cords 81,112,113
doeskins 113
druggets 33,34,*36*,40
duffles 54
flannel . . . 33,39,40,55,80
kerseys 23,39
liveries 54,55,99,113
meltons 113
moleskins 113
plunkets 26,31,54
osetes 17
rays 17
Salisbury 43,55
serges 34,39,40,
80,100
Spanish 31,32,33,34,
35,39,76
superfines . . . 54,55,74,77
toilinettes 54
tweeds 113,119
Venetians 113
Cloths sent to Bristol
Fair *61*
Clothier's houses *38*
Stock-in-trade *43*
Cockayne,
Sir William 31
Cockell family 53,54
Cogswell, Edward *29*
Jacob 110
James 112,120
Coleford, Somerset 47
Colerne, Wiltshire . . . 40,52
Coley, Avon 23
Collicott and Co. 77
Collier, William 110

Compton, John 25
Cook family 53,67,69,
Cooper family . . . 34,64,81,
99,101
John *93*
Corsley, Wiltshire . . . 47,54,
75,76,84,85,104
Coulthurst, Matthew . . . 64
Courtney and Co. 81
Courts Mill *95,96,115*
Cradle Bridge factories,
Trowbridge *104*
Cray, Jeremiah 48
Crockerton,
Wiltshire 50,76,100
Cullurne, Joseph 74
Daniell,
Joseph Clisild 102
Dauntsey, Wiltshire 48
Davis family 47,53
Davison, Henry 32
Deacon, Thomas 99
Defoe, Daniel 35,36,
40,43
Devizes, Wiltshire 21,
24,26,33,40,41,43,47,50,
52,63,68,69,76,80,81,
84,100
Dicks, J. and Son . . . 109,119
Dilton Marsh,
Wiltshire 75,103,112
Dowding family 53,110
Down, Ann 47
Downton, Wiltshire 17
Draper, John 20
Duchman, Corner, burial
of *36*
Dunkerton, Henry 20
Dunkirk factory *75*
Dursley,
Gloucestershire . . . 39,48
Dutch immigrants . . . 33,34,
48
dyehouses *46,56,57,103*
dye-recipe book *46*
Dyer, Edward 120
John 82,102
dyestuffs 14,21,23,47
Edington, Wiltshire 32
Edmunds family 101,
113
Edridge,
Abraham Lloyd 76
Elcot in Marlborough,
Wiltshire 17,69
Elderton, James 53,54,
55,*61*,63
embezzlement 62,64
Everett family 40,52,
53,76
Exeter 47
Farleigh Hungerford,
Somerset . . . 20,21,28,52,
109,113,122
Mill *125*

Fastolf, Sir John..... 18,20
Figheldean, Wiltshire... 81
Fisher family......... 110
Fisherton, Wiltshire.... 80, 82
Flower family........ 26
Ford, John........ 68,73
France............ 31,68
Freshford, Avon.... 28,32, 75,76,82,84,104,109,110, 112,119, mill............ *90*
Frome, Somerset...... 18 passim
Literary and Scientific Institute........ *117*
Fulling mill........ *19,27*
Gabriel, J.W..... 120,121
Gaby, William........ 34
Gaisford, William..... 84
Gaite, William........ 99
Gane, Richard....... 112
Gatford, John........ 21
Gayton, Abraham..... 110
Germany..... 26,28,31,68
Goldney family.. 34,41,42
Gousborough, Mr...... 53
Grant, Edmund....... 52
Greenland Upper Mill............ *79,114*
Greene, Isaac......... 41
Greystone House, Devizes............. *38*
Guppy and Armstrong......... 69
Haden, George..... 82,*98*
Haley, Abraham...... 110
Hall, A.R......... 16
Hall family......... 53
Halwey family........ 20
Hams, Harry..... 109,113
Hanson and Mills... 54,55
Hargreaves, James..... 67
Harmer, John........ 69
Harnham, West, Wiltshire...... 17,81,84
Harper, Taylor and Little......... 112,120
Harptree, Avon..... 36,40
Harrop family....... 109, 112,120
Hart, Samuel......... 99
Hawkeridge Mill..... *123*
Hawkins, Geoffrey..... 28
Haynes, William...... 20
Hayward, J & E... 120,121
Heath, Ralph........ 78
Heaven, Samuel...... 68
heddle and slay maker............ *108*
Hewitt family.... 113,120
Hewlett, John........ 55
Heytesbury, Wiltshire... 21, 23,52,53,67,76,84,100 101,103,104,113
Hill, Francis........ 74,76

Hilliker, Thomas.... 78,79
Hillman, Stephen... *38*,43, 47,50,52
Hilperton, Wiltshire... *38,* 40,68,81,110
Hinchcliffe, George... 110
Hinxman, Hussey and Co.......... 80,81
Hoep, Mathias....... 28
Holland........ 26,28,31
Holroyd, James...... 110
Holt, Wiltshire..... 40,76, 84,104,113,121
Home Mill...... *115,125*
Hopkins and Howard......... 99
Horningsham, Wiltshire..... 40,48,*49,* 52,76
horse power........ 73,81
Horton family..... 21,24, 26,40
Houlton family.... 34,35, 40,42
Houston and Son.... 109, 112,113,122
Hungerford family.... 20, 21
Huntley, John........ 54
Hussey, William....... 42
Hutchins, William..... 80
Iford in Westwood, Wiltshire..... 24,28,75
Irish, John.......... 26
Jarvis, Thomas...... 82
Jenkins and Green..... 76
Jenkins, William....... 77
Jervis family....... 42,80
Jesser family...... 34,48, 53,73
Jones, John... 76,78,79,80
Joyce, Cooper and Co............. 99
Keevil, Wiltshire.... 18,20, 21,24,26,*27*
Kemp family..... 120,121
Keynsham, Avon... 23,47, 68,74,110
Kingston Mill......... 79
Kintbury, Berkshire.... 69
Kitson, Thomas....... 23
Knook, Wiltshire....... 55
Lacy, Simon.......... 21
Langford family..... 24,28
Langham in Rode, Somerset......... 28,75
Laverton family... 109,113, 119,120
Lavington, Market, Wiltshire........... 21
Ledyard, Samuel...... 53
Leland, John......... 23
Leigh-on-Mendip, Somerset......... 21
Limpley Stoke, Wiltshire..... 28,76,101, 102,109

Littleton, Avon........ 40
Littleton in Semington, Wiltshire..... 21,24,78
Litton, Avon......... 40
London... 18,21,23,25,26, 28,31,32,33,34,42,43,47, 48,53,55,112
Long family..... 24,26,28, 40,43,48
Robert.......... 20
Thomas, pattern book of............. *43,*43
cloth making book.......... *58*
Lovell, Thomas....... 20
Lucas, Walter........ 20
Luccombe Mill....... 77
Lullington, Somerset... 17, 28,32,50,84
machine makers....... *71*
machines
carding machine... 48,67, 68,69,*70*,73,74,75,76, 99,110
cutter...... 102,111,*135*
fly-shuttle.... 76,83,112
fulling stocks... *15*,15,16, 67,74,84,102,*138*
gig-mill... 25,28,52,67, *72*,74,76,77,78,79,82,84, *98*,102
mule..... 101,102,110, 111,*130*
power loom.... 102,103
reel............. 49,*58*
scribbling machine... 34, 69,73,74,75,76,99,110
shearing frame... 69,*72,* 74,77,78,79,82, 84,102,111
slubbing billy.... 68,69, *70*,110
spinning jenny... 67,68, 69,*70*,73,74,80,110
timmy nog.......... 51
vertical loom........ *12*
willey........... 48,67
Magill and Stephens...... 109,113
Malmesbury, Wiltshire... 23,24,26,32, 40,48,74,76,77,83,84, 101,104,109
Manchester........... 35
marks of clothiers... 28,*29,* 30,32,34,53
Marlborough, Wiltshire...... 14,15,69
Matravers and Overbury... 100,109,110
Matthew, James....... 48
May family........ 26,79
Meech, Thomas Luke....... 74
Melksham, Wiltshire... 28, 34,40,43,48,52,55,*56*,63,

68,74,75,81,84,99,101, 104,110,113,121
Mells, Somerset..... 21,23
Menders, Salters........ *3*
Merchant Adventurers... 28,31,32
Mere, Wiltshire..... 18,40
Methuen family..... 33,34, 35,43
Michell family........ 26
Milford, Wiltshire..... 50, 80,81
Millard and Sons..... 110
Minety, Wiltshire...... 48
Mitchell, Mr.......... 80
Moggridge and Joyce......... 74,76,*90*
Moore and Edmunds...... 112,119
Morris, Samuel....... 110
Mortimer family.... 40,55
Mundy, Samuel...... 101
Naish family.... 68,78,81
Nemnich, P.A........ 80
New Park Street, Devizes............. *86*
Newbury, Berkshire... 23,24
Northampton......... 26
Norton Bavant, Wiltshire........ 26,28
Norton St. Philip, Somerset........... 24
Nunny, Somerset..... 52
Ogden, James........ 68
Oil, Gallipoli......... 48
Oseney, Oxfordshire... 24
Palmer and McKays... 112
Passion, Anthony...... 24
family........... 28
pattern books.... *43,* 43
Peach, Benjamin....... 53
Pearce, Nicholas....... 40
Pennsylvania, U.S.A.... 55
Pensford, Avon.. 23,28,36
Pewsey, Wiltshire..... 112
Phelps family.... 40,69,73
Philps, William....... 20
Pitman, W. and T...... 53
Samuel......... 101
Pitton, Wiltshire....... 48
Portugal............. 68
Pottern, Wiltshire..... 26
Potticary family........ 26
Poulshot, Wiltshire.... 76, 100
Prangley, Thomas...... 67
processes:
burling.... 49,50,*58,136*
braying........... 111
carding....... 16,34,48, 80,*129,130*
drawing........... *132*
dyeing....... 47,48,*129*
fulling....... 49,50,59, 75,*135*

picking 47
quill winding *134*
raising 51,52
scouring 13,14,15,
            48,50,111
scribbling 33,48,80
shearing 52,53
sorting *128*
spinning *12,16*,48,49
tenter-rack *59*
warping 13,49,*131*
washing *134*
weaving 13,*133*
Pyard, Christopher 26,
    family 28
Pyke, Thomas 67
Queen Camel,
    Somerset 36
Quemerford in Calne,
    Wiltshire 28,*81*,101
Quidhampton,
    Wiltshire 80,81
Rawlings and Gregory . . . 48
    H.J. & Co. 122
Rawlings and Pocock . . . 110
Ray, Robert 28
Read family 54,79
riots . . . 64,65,69,76,81,100
Rode, Somerset 28,40,
    54,68,73,80,82,84,85,
    104,109,122
Rodgers family 110
Rossiter family 109
Russell, N.C. 16
Sadler, Robert 68
Sage, William 52
Salisbury, Wiltshire 17,
    21,23,24,26,28,33,39,40,
    41,42,48,50,55,67,69,73,
    76,80,81,101,102
Salisbury family 68,69
Salter family 43,103,
    104,112,113,119,120,
    121,122,*137*
    Samuel *117*
Saunders and Fanner . . . 82
Scott family 34
Scottish trade 119
Scutts Bridge Mill *125*
Seagry, Wiltshire 53
sealing of cloth *19*, 50
Seend, Wiltshire 20,39,
    43,49,80,*87*
    Church *22*
Selfe family 34
Selwood Road,
    Frome *33*
Serle, John 48
Sewey, William 21

Shawford in Beckington,
    Somerset 28,109,
               111,121
Shearmen *60*
Sheppard, family . . . 41,53,
    76,78,83,109,
    113,119,120
Sheppards Barton,
    Frome *35*
Shepton Mallet,
    Somerset . . 31,32,34,*37*,
    39,40,47,48,55,67,77,78,
    80,84,99,100,101
    silk manufacture 69,81,
               99,100
Silver Street Factory,
    Trowbridge *86*
Sinkins, John *117*
Sinkins and Wood 109,
               113
Smith family 34
Symthe, John 23
Snap-reel, The Snap'd 45
Southwick, Wiltshire . . . 26,
               103
Spring Gardens, Frome,
    Somerset . . . 24,28,84,*94*,
    109,119,120,*122*
Stancomb and
    Wilkins 109,113
Stanley in Calne,
    Wiltshire 17
Staverton, Wiltshire . . . 28,
    76,78,79,80,83,84,*91*99,
    101,110,111,113,*124*
steam power 76,81,82,
    84,*94*,*101*,103,104,110
Stephens, Lawrence 21
Stevens and Bailward . . . 47
Stillman, Thomas 84
Stockton, Wiltshire 26
Stoddart and Co. 99
Stoke Lane, Avon 23
Stokes, John 20
Stone Mill *93*
Stone, William 31
Stowford in Wingfield,
    Wiltshire 21,24,
    28,*29*,75
    mill *58*
Stowford, William 21
Stadbrook mill *127*
strike, 1829 . . . . *101*
Strode family 32,34,
Strang and Webber 85
Studley Mill *4*,*53*,*114*
Stumpe, William 24
Suppliers to
    factories *106*

Swindon, Wiltshire 48
Talboys House *27*
Tanner, William 110
Tarrant, Uriah 76
Taunton,
    John Hooper 75,76
teazles 14,21,51,52,
               59,102
Tellisford, Somerset . . . 28,75
    mill *51*
Temple family 40,42
Temple, William . . . 40,55,
              64,*66*
Terumber, James 21
Tetbury,
    Gloucestershire 26
Tinhead in Edington,
    Wiltshire 25,26,28
Tisbury, Wiltshire 80
Topp family 26
Towker, James 20,21
Trowbridge Cottage
    Hospital *118*
Trowbridge, Wiltshire . . . 18
    passim 103,105,107,
    108,114,116,118
truck 63,64,100,102
Tucker, John 85
    Josiah 65
    W.H. 112
Twerton, Avon 18,28,
    68,74,77,78,84,*88*,102,
    104,109,110,113,122
    Upper Mill *93*
Udall, Joseph 40
Unions *91*100
Upton Lovell Mill *83*

Usher and Jeffries 43,
               47,55
Vine, Thomas 75,76
Viveash and Co. 84
Waldron family 42,
              74,75
Walker family 54,120
Wallbridge mill *115*
Wallis family 28
Wansey family . . . 34,*36*,*37*,
    40,42,48,50,52,55,63,
    69,76,82,99
Warminster,
    Wiltshire 21,34,*36*,
    37,40,41,*44*,54,73,77,
    78,79,80,84,99
Wastfield family 82
Waterford Factory 97
Waterford mill *125*,*138*
Water driven
    factories *87*,*88*,*93*

Watt, James 68,82
Watts family 53,55
Waylen family 109
Weavers' Cottage,
    Seend *87*
weavers' houses *107*
weaving shops *106*,*108*
    sheds *114*
Weavers' Union mug . . . *11*
Webb, Benedict 31
    J.H. & Sons 120
Wells, Somerset 21,23
West Lavington *27*
Westbury, Wiltshire 20
    passim 105
    House, Bradford *41*
Westbury Leigh,
    Wiltshire . . . 18,*29*,68,69,
    74,75,109,112
    mill *89*
Westley, William 55
Weston near Bath,
    Avon 17,*88*
Westwood, Wiltshire . . . 21,
    24,25,26,74
Whaddon, Wiltshire . . . 18,
    26,28
Wheeler family 82
Whelpley, Thomas 25
White, William *43*
Whitaker family 25,
    26,28
Whiting, John 40
Wilkins family 28,53,
    54,109
Willow Vale, Frome *87*
Wilton, Wiltshire 23,
    76,81
Winchcombe, John 23,
               24
Winterslow, Wiltshire . . . 48
Wither, Anthony 32
Woodlands, West,
    Somerset 76
Woods, Mr, steam engine
    maker 81
Worcester 34
Workshops *57*,*86*,*87*
Wraxall, North,
    Wiltshire 52
    South, Wiltshire . . . 40
Wykes, John 20,21
Yatesbury, Wiltshire 48
Yatton 26
Yerbury family 23,24,
    26,28,32,39,41,43,
    50,51,*116*
Yorkshire trade 39,54,
              76,77

ENDPAPERS: FRONT: Trowbridge factories; BACK: map of the woollen
industry districts of Wiltshire and Somerset.

Subscribers

Presentation Copies

1 Wiltshire County Council
2 Somerset County Council
3 Wiltshire Library Service
4 Somerset Library Service
5 Avon Library Service
6 Wiltshire County Records Office
7 Trowbridge Museum
8 Devizes Museum
9 Chippenham Museum
10 Frome Museum
11 Kenneth Hudson
12 John Naish

13 K.H.Rogers
14 Clive & Carolyn Birch
15 Alan Andrew
16 Agnes MacLeav
17 Barbara R.Booth
18 R.Webster
19 Mrs C.E.Newton
20 Wiltshire Folk Life Society
21 Mrs Grace Marsden
22 E.J.Lanfear
23 Margaret Adams
24 Mr & Mrs D.L. Johnston
25 Somerset County Library
31
32 G.M.Land-Reeves
33 Clare W.Higgens
34 B.R.Rogers
35 Mr & Mrs C.J. Kelsey
36 G.W.Hibberd
37 Mary J.Harris
38 Miss B.M.Austin
39 Victoria & Albert Museum
40 London Guildhall Library
41 Commander A.S. Craig OBE RN
42 Nicholas Plant
43 Kate Sykes
44 K.& R.Charles
45 Mrs Eunice Hillman
46 Nicol Smith
47 Urchfont Manor College
48 Audrey Hirst
49 Mrs L.Young
50 Miss A.Marjorie Jackson
51 Godfrey F.Laurence
52 Robert Harvey
53 Mrs M.Dauncey
54 Mr & Mrs E.Curtis
55 Mrs Audrey Charles
56 Desmond Patrick Rowe
57 Miss Jean M. Applegate
58 Gee Langdon
59 John H.Harvey
60 Mrs M.J.Webb
61 University of Bristol, Extra Mural Library
62 Miss B.Morris
63 Pamela Leah
64 Derryn A.Copley
65 A.D.Stephens
66 J.R.Tanner
67 Noel Knee
68 Jane Whinney
69 Miss M.E.Orchard
70 Rodney D.Goodall
71 Patricia Bruton
72 Mrs Pearl Holden
73 Rev E.Hurst

74 Roger F.Mawby
75 David & Wende Maunder
76 Catherine M.Baldwin
77 Mrs Margaret Freer
78 Brian J.Murless
79 Mrs P.M.Hembry
80 Raymond F.Alder
81 J.B.McDonald
82 Harold Fassnidge
83 Dr.P.F.Parker
84 M.J.Hodgson
85 T.A.Barrett-Grey
86 K.J.Appleton
87 O.F.Brown
88 B.C.Wheeler
89 Hugh Francis Seymour
90 Lt Cmdr R.J. Cogswell
91 A.J.W.Stancomb
92 L.V.Bowring
93 Roy Hillcoat
94 David G.James
95 I.D.Burgess
96 Paul & Shirley Nicholls
97 D.J.Pollard
98 County of Avon
99 Mrs K.M.Houlton
100 Wiltshire Guild of Spinners, Weavers & Dyers
101 Nancy Pollard
102 H.Futcher
103 Mrs J.M.Bradley
104 Mr & Mrs A.J. Garner
105 Graham Andrew
106 Caroline Andrew
107 Mrs D.W.J.Skull
108 Mrs Christine Moore
109 T.E.Morland
110 Mrs D.A.Holton
111 B.M.Willmott Dobbie
112 Percy Hale

113 C.A.Buchanan
114 John Tyrrell
115 Mrs G.Coveney
116
117 Derek Pomeroy
118 Mrs E.M.Doncaster
119 Doreen Burford
120 Rosemary Anne MacGregor
121 D.M.Anderson
122 J.R.Broome
123 Mr & Mrs P.Q. Treloar
124 R.P.de B Nicholson
125 Mrs H.J.Ames
126 Michael Charles Morris
127 Geoffrey Lancashire
128 Mr & Mrs John Hignett
129 Somerset County Library
134
135 M.Cleveland
136 Mrs Janet Lindsay Repton
137 Yvonne Cole
138 Hugh Phillips
139 Mrs Margaret Martin
140 Joyce Purcell
141 Mr & Mrs M.H. Statham
142 John Landell Mills
143 Mrs G.M.King
144 Miss F.A.Raybould
145 Donald Napier Corbyn
146 A.D.Stevens
147 Mrs P.M.Asby
148 M.Spater/M.Scott
149 Mr & Mrs D.J. Bonney
150 Viola Hale
151 Mrs F.M.Lawton
152 Nicholas Plant
153 Edward Plant
154 James Plant
155 Geoffrey Banner

156 Prof C.R.Tottle
157 Grace Fairhurst
158 Eric W.Mattock
159 Mrs M.Oram
160 K.C.G.Heath
161 Edward Bradby
162 Roger Mussell
163 School Library
165 Service, Bridgwater
166 H.E.Gunstone
167 Derek Prosser
168 R.B.Hillman
169 Miss M.Joyce Gibbs
170 Tony Bullen
171 Robert Oglesby
172 C.H.H.Harwood
173 Ronald Grant
174 F.J.Seward
175 R.G.Burgess
176 Terence A.Birch
177 R.C.Wilkins
178 Dennis Gardner
179 Margaret E.Stacey
180 Charles H.Burgess
181 Jeanne M.Castle
182 J.B.Walsby
183 A.MacLeay
184 R.A.Phillips
185 Keith Falconer
186 Mrs P.M.Slocombe
187 H.J.Hampson
188 Miss M.C.Hanks
189 Mr & Mrs R.B. Witcomb
190 M.Berry
191 Chester College Library
192 Elizabeth Butler
193 Mrs S.R.Bacon
194 W.G.Appleby
195 Audrey R.Heeley (Williton)
196 K.V.Bryce
197 E.J.Stevens
198 Myrtle Pratten
199 Patricia Gosling
200 Frank Edward Sweet
201 Malcolm John Sweet
202 P.B.Thomas
203 Keith A.Hartley
204 Matthew Cory
205 Newtown Junior School
206 Anthony Houghton-Brown
207 A.J.Carter
208 Mrs Dora Ahl
209 R.A.& B.J.Buchanan
210 Janet C.Ruddick
211 Stephen Hurd
212 R.F.Andrews
213 William Harry John Fox
214 Miss M.E.Pearce
215 A.S.White
216 William Jenkin Davies
217 Miss J.M.Pippet
218 R.Brigden

219 John d'Arcy
220 Arnold & Jo Elvidge
221 Mrs J. Neville
222 Peggy Sugden
223 M. Mines
224 Mrs J. M. Morrison
225 Geoffrey Short
226 G. H. Scobie
227 B. P. A. Daines
228 J. H. Bettey
229 M. E. Jones
230 Vernon Gibbs
231 Nancy Wise
232 W. G. M. Angliss
233 Mrs D. J. Hodgkiss
234 Elizabeth Botting
235 S. B. Murrin
236 Paul A. Blake
237 Harold Saunders
238 R. L. W. Moon
239 Mrs Janet Hall
240 A. H. Francis
241 Donald Box
242 M. E. Stacey
243 Christine Hillier
244 Roma Mearles Ware
245 Mrs Barbara Wallis
246 P. H. Bowerman
247 R. MacDonald Smith
248 Brenda & David
    Eldridge
249 Joan Day
250 Barbara Croucher
251 R. Bennett
252 W. J. Petch
253 W. & V. Chadwick
254 Dr A. D. Cox
255 R. Ruddle
256 C. J. Mitchell
257 E. Moore
258 M. J. Stone
259 Ronald W. Foxwell
260 Dr C. A. Shell
261 North Star Library
262 Downside Abbey
    Library
263 Miss Alison Franklin
264 Mrs Mary Harris
265 Jean Houldey
266 G. M. Slade
267 Miss M. M. Smith
268 R. T. Mitchell
269 Mrs Betty Smith
270 Wiltshire Library
297 Service
298 N. E. M. Davies
299 Nancy Steele
300 M. J. Lansdown
301 Kathleen & Marjorie
    Reeves
302 R. I. E. Haynes
303 J. A. & K. E. Couldridge
304 Miss Olive P. Sharp
305 D. J. Turner
306 F. & N. Gunthorp
307 Hugh Seymour
308 Joan Aslett
309 Patricia Tidy

310 Anthony J. Boult
311 Glyn Bridges
312 Mrs Harriet James
313 G. H. Johnston
314 Marion Dutch
315 Joyce Meineke
316 Jim Denning
317 Bud Fuller
318 Mr & Mrs Andrew
    Jones
319 Mr & Mrs Peter
    Martin
320 W. F. London
321 Eileen M. Curtis
322 Bernard M. Pearce
323 Mr & Mrs P. S. W. Beard
324 Mrs M. Jump
325 John & Myra Gander
326 Adrian C. Powell
327 Derek Gill
328 Miss J. M. Johnson
329 Chris G. D. Penny
330 Mr & Mrs G. B.
    Mitchell
331 Alan Crudge
332 Mrs K. M. Houlton
333 R. J. Aplin
334 M. W. Redgrave
335 P. A. Boyce
336 Steve Lovering
337 John Curtis
338 T. W. J. Lovell
339 Dominic Aiden
    Bellenger
340 Mrs Isobel Ponting
341 Norman J. Rogers
342 Wiltshire County
    Council
343 Frank & Jean
    Dummett
344 Derek Thomas
345 Mrs K. G. Atkins
346 Peter W. H. Pickup
347 Josephine Jacobs
348 Hilda Massey
349 Mrs S. M. Selwyn-Smith
350 H. A. Druett
351 Mrs M. E. Mason
352 Mr Shields
353 David Kelly
354 Mrs M. F. Simms
355 Andrew Houghton
356 Yvonne Elizabeth
    Marsh
357 Mrs L. J. Hale
358
    Pat White
360
361 R. Edwards
362 Molly Hopkins
363 Mrs M. Clark
364 N. G. Withey
365 Mr & Mrs B. K.
    Wenham
366 D. C. J. Maidment
367 Mrs E. K. Maidment
368 Mrs A. Commander
369 Eileen Jennings
370 D. Gilson

371 Doreen & Ted
    Appleby
372 Roger F. Newman
373 G. M. J. Parsons
374 Mrs E. Kamm
375 P. A. Boyce
376 Trevor Porter
377 Mr & Mrs L. I.
    Mintowt-Czyz
378 Mr & Mrs J. Fielding
379 Iris Heald
380 Susan Leighton
381 C. W. Franklin
382 R. J. Titt
383 Mrs M. I. Moles
384 Mrs A. R. Wilson
385 Edward Rogers
386 Anthony Rogers
387 Tom Rogers
388 Harold Coward
389 Kathy Lewis
390 Miss M. P. Campbell
391 G. H. Nicholls
392 L. M. Noad
393 Tutor-Librarian, Bath
    Academy of Art
394 Miss M. I. Hale
395 W. J. & S. Berry
396 Keith A. Moore
397 Dorna A. Daw
398 J. R. Boyne-Aitken
399 M. E. Balston
400 Mrs M. O. Holland
401 E. Moore
402 Frome College
    (Further Education)
403 Miss M. Campbell
404 R. G. Hoare
405 P. Harding
406 Aubrey Winter
407 Miss K. G. Forbes
408 Rev C. F. Sweet
409 Paul E. Pickering
410 Mr & Mrs R. J. Platts
411 Michael McGarvie
412 David & Ann Mattock
413 John of Gaunt
414 School
415 Alan Reginald Newth
416 John Sawtell
417 Avon Antiques,
    Bradford on Avon
418 John Chandler
419 Mrs G. Martin
420 M. Breakspear
421 Evelyn Jenkins
422 Dr C. A. Minty
423 Mrs Roma Challis
424 G. W. Damsell
425 J. H. B. Hornby
426 Rear Admiral D. G.
427 Titford
428 Leonard Fare
429 Mrs D. Bryant
430 Mrs M. Graham
431 Steven Rees
432 M. E. Ashton
433 Miss J. A. Fletcher

434 Kenneth W. Farr
435 I. D. Clark
436 Mrs Delia Kingsbury
437 G. H. Butcher
438 B. H. Butcher
439 G. M. Gumm
440 Dudley B. Cradock
441 E. J. Hiscock
442 Joyce & Jack Carter
443 Mr & Mrs John
    Beresford
444 R. O'Brien
445 Mr & Mrs Ivan Taylor
446 Mrs M. E. Westerman
447 Ralf Lamsdale
448 Miss A. E. Tadd
449 R. A. Pearce
450 Mrs Mary C. Harper
451 Miss F. Bushell
452 Frank Martin
453 Mrs M. P. R. Purnell
454 J. M. Snook
455
456 Mrs Lystra M. Berrett
457 Michael C. Reynolds
458 Mrs Rosemary
    Bridgeman
459 Heather Tanner
460 Mrs Margaret Lyndsell
461 G. A. Kingsbury
462 P. A. Alner
463 Dr I. G. Elloway
464 Michael Marshman
465 Warminster History
    Society
466 Jack Field
467 Andrew Houghton
468 Jean Davis
469 Mrs Joanne Land
470 R. Brebner
471 Mrs E. M. Mead
472 Mrs E. E. M. Randall
473 Mrs K. C. White
474 V. Carter
475 Mrs L. McGill
476
477 Mrs D. Driscoll
478 Mrs F. Day
479 F. H. Smith
480 Mrs D. M. Owen
481 Michael Lloyd
482 Mary Salisbury
483 Mrs G. C. Elkins
484 Mrs M. Fivash
485 Mrs R. A. Clark
486 W. G. Manners
487 John Challicom
488 Jean Shuttleworth
489 M. Neate
490 C. E. MacLoed-Iles
491 W. G. Wilhams
492 Mrs Jean Shuttleworth
493 Mrs P. A. Cook
494 Roy Sampson
495 Miss F. M. Crook
496 Mrs J. Earnshaw

Remaining names unlisted